Servanthood

Servanthood

Leadership for
the Third Millennium

Bennett J. Sims

Wipf & Stock
PUBLISHERS
Eugene, Oregon

Wipf and Stock Publishers
199 W 8th Ave, Suite 3
Eugene, OR 97401

Servanthood
Leadership for the Third Millennium
By Sims, Bennett J.
Copyright©1997 by Sims, Bennett J.
ISBN: 1-59752-075-6
Publication date 2/1/2005
Previously published by Cowley Publications, 1997

For Three Stalwart Servant Leaders

Edmond Lee Browning, 1929–
Presiding Bishop of the Episcopal Church, USA,
New York, New York
compassionate pastor and courageous captain of a church
sailing the heavy seas of momentous cultural change
and divisive internal stress

James Wilson Rouse, 1914-1996
Founder of The Rouse Company and
The Enterprise Foundation, both of Columbia, Maryland
visionary ground-breaker in the management of American
business, for whom the bottom line was always the quality of
company relationships, and whose commitment to the poor
was a foremost personal concern

Willis W. Harman, 1918-1997
President Emeritus of the Institute of Noetic Sciences
Sausalito, California
scientist, educator, and seer, a practitioner of servanthood in
several careers, who saw contemporary science leading the
way to a recovery of "spirit" as fundamental to a scientifically
accurate world-view, which he called "global mind change"

Table of Contents

Velvet and Steel

This book seeks to integrate the religious and secular dimensions of life in a fresh understanding of power. Servanthood is a proper term for the integration, but it needs a sturdier definition than either religion or the secular order usually give it. From the religious standpoint, "servanthood" tends to mean a lofty ideal, all right for Sunday school classes and the Boy Scout movement, but isolated from the so-called real world of win/lose competition. From the secular perspective "servanthood" often means "servitude," a condition either imposed on women and racially different groups by male-dominant cultures, or self-imposed by both men and women out of fear of their own power.

This book aims to recover for servanthood its power to transform human experience and, in consequence, the character of God's interwoven world. I will argue that servanthood is the way of fulfilling the human longing for peace and the planet's need of preservation as the theater of all life. Servanthood is the name for the quality of leadership that is needed to secure the world as we move into the third millennium. Servant power functions as a two-way exchange, never as subjugating dominance; it not only influences others, but is also open to influence. Servanthood acknowledges and respects the freedom of another and seeks to enhance the other's capacity to make a difference. Wherever such leadership is exercised—at home, at work, in business and the church, in the classroom and throughout the globe—it can result in an astonishing increase in zest, creativity, productivity and, best of all, in bonding people into communities of caring. This is the "velvet and steel" of servant leadership, a mystical blend of gentleness and strength. It is a paradox that gains by giving.

The emergence of servanthood as a way of leading represents a new hold on the old truth that greatness lies in serving (Mark 10:35-45). It coincides with the leading edges of a vast turning point in human history, a sea-change of greater magnitude than any since the agricultural revolution ten thousand years ago that inaugurated the use of human power to manipulate and exploit the earth. More and more we see the futility of "superpower" politics and its reliance on domination, threat, weaponry, and violence as problem-solvers. The atomic bomb cracked open the door to this perception; the unchecked advance of human population and industrial plunder has thrown it wide open. Slowly, very slowly, the value of caring for one another and for the earth gains the respect of the powerful. For their leadership of the world, made increasingly one, they need the supportive "velvet and steel" of millions at all levels of human leading, from parenting to presiding. They need plain people committed to the enduring power of love.

Love appears to have been here since the dawn of human consciousness, but contemporary science would go much further back in the history of the universe to speculate on love's antiquity. Teilhard de Chardin, the French Jesuit paleontologist, building on molecular bonding as an empirical reality, developed a view which quantum physics now ratifies. Quantum theorists are certain that there is a caring pulse of energy that animates and interconnects all the entities in the cosmos. Teilhard put his speculation outrageously for his time: "Molecules make love." For this statement, and others like it, his church's hierarchy banned the publication of his books. But time has moved many hearts. Progressive thinkers in all contemporary fields now know and favor what Teilhard pioneered as a scientist theologian. Molecules do make love—or something akin to it—in their compulsion to reach for one another in creating the communities we call living organisms.

This book travels even further back in time than quantum theory to find the origins of the concept. The scriptures of one of the world's faith communities locate its roots in God. Writing of Jesus, his criminal execution and resurrected life, St. Paul declared, "We proclaim Christ crucified, a stumbling block to Jews and foolishness to Gentiles, but to those who are called, both Jews and Greeks, Christ the *power of God and the wisdom of God* (1 Corinthians 1:23-24, italics mine). This is the two-way exchange of wise power that undergirds all that is, the velvet and steel of enduring love: gentle enough to cradle the cosmos in patient care and strong enough to outlast and forgive all assaults on its compassion.

∞

Many people have contributed to the making of this book, particularly Robert K. Greenleaf, who died in 1990 but who continues to accompany me like a personal angel. First among others of importance is Mary Page Sims, best friend, wife, and collaborator. Gordon Cosby, founder of the Church of the Savior in Washington, D.C., was the first person with whom I shared the dream of starting the Institute for Servant Leadership many years ago. Barbara Brown Taylor, distinguished preacher and author, has read nearly every word, nudging me to subtract here and add there. James C. Fenhagen, author and former Dean and President of The General Theological Seminary, also has given me critical encouragement. Alan Anderson, writer, editor, and fellow-searcher, has spent countless hours weeding the tangled garden of these scribblings and helping to make it a tidier patch. Parker J. Palmer, renowned teacher, author, and colleague in hope, has also read portions of the manuscript and clarified my thoughts.

Others I would like to thank include Jim L. Waits, former Dean of the Candler School of Theology of Emory University, and James T. Laney, former President of Emory. Without their support the Institute for Servant Leadership and its worldwide ministry would not exist. In 1995 the Archbishop of Canterbury, Dr. George Carey, invited me to address a meeting of the three dozen primates (chief pastors) of the Anglican Communion around the world. Two of the addresses I presented at that meeting prepared the way for this book. Finally, I am grateful to the Board of Directors of the Institute for Servant Leadership, who have prodded me for several years to put into writing what they and I believe about leadership as Christians. We are to Archbishop Carey what seeds are to the sower, and God gave the increase.

Part 1

∞

The Meaning of
Servant Leadership

Chapter 1

"I See You"

*For you I am a bishop, but with you I am a Christian. The
first is an office accepted; the second is a gift received. One
is danger; the other is safety. If I am happier to be redeemed
with you than to be placed over you, then I shall, as the Lord
commanded, be more fully your servant.*

—Augustine of Hippo

A single moment can be pivotal in a person's life. Such a
moment overturns old ways of seeing the world and
begins an inner pilgrimage that beckons in a new direction.
This happened to me on August 28, 1963 in Washington, D.C.
That decade was pivotal for so many of my generation in
America; it acted like a long heat wave on our hearts. Because
the same sun hardens clay and melts ice, some hearts were
hardened and some were softened. I do not know the "why"
of this difference. I only know the joy of my own good fortune
in having the sun's intensity soften my heart and open my
eyes.

Or maybe it was the other way around—first seeing and
then feeling a new sensation. The pivotal day began in Baltimore at 7:30 in the morning, when more than seventy people
from around the city gathered for worship in my parish

church, the Episcopal Church of the Redeemer. The service had been announced some time before as an appeal to church members who wished to go by bus to the nation's capital for the March on Washington. Our special intention in that service was to offer the day's event for God's blessing, asking that it be used to advance the kingdom which the church routinely (and perhaps thoughtlessly) presses heaven to install on earth. We also prayed that the day would be so presided over by God's Spirit that it would bring credit to the cause of social justice, move the hearts of many, and keep those of us who participated in the march from judging those who ignored or resisted it.

Following worship we gathered in the church parking lot to board two waiting buses. Also waiting for us was a man who had summoned the police to watch from lurking patrol cars and who, with a helper, pressed letters of protest upon each of us. Undeterred, we accepted the letters, boarded the buses, and headed for the Baltimore-Washington Parkway. Traffic began to thicken about ten miles above the District line. We were passed by a number of silver monsters, all bearing bright banners tied below the bus windows. One of them read: PILGRIM BAPTIST CHURCH, BROOKLYN, NEW YORK. MARCH ON WASHINGTON. They had left their homes before dawn.

By the time we entered the city from the northeast the buses had clustered four abreast, using both inbound and outbound lanes. We were a tidal wave of thundering vehicles, churning bumper to bumper through the dense black residential area along New York Avenue. Police preparation had cleared the streets of all traffic. A strange silence had settled over that part of the city, broken only by the diesel growl of the buses. As a close observer of two communist-led demonstrations in Tokyo in 1962 I had felt the threatening explosiveness of tense public quiet. By contrast, the mid-morning hush along New York Avenue that day seemed like an expectant reverence.

Scattered in clusters along the curb were black children, most of them waving. Under the rules of the march children under fourteen were excluded. So they greeted the hundreds of buses from street-side, all scrubbed and polished for the event. Some even danced, the white flounces on the little girls' frocks bouncing up and down in the morning sun. Their faces were aglow, like the shining faces of children anywhere in the world when transfigured by an uncomprehended joy.

The caravan turned a sharp corner and swung close to the curb. There, not ten feet from the bus window against which I was seated, stood a large black woman of middle years, her feet planted wide, her arms raised up and out in a vast gesture of welcome, her head thrown back, her cheeks awash in tears, her face radiant. In that instant I saw a human soul in all its majesty, in all its beauty of suffering, forbearance, and longing, a human soul like mine. In that instant I knew that all the noble words we used in religion and the defining documents of American freedom—all the careful, cloistered words of resolution, all the pious Christian words about the equality and worth of every human person—in that instant I knew those words were true. At last I believed them. And I was thrilled to the core to be on that bus, ashamed of my complicity in that woman's humiliation, transported with the joy of deliverance from a smothering prejudice that had imprisoned and stunted my soul for forty-three years. As a society we are imprisoned still—less so today, I believe, but with "miles to go before we sleep." The secret of my release from prejudicial bondage lay in the unbidden gift of seeing deeply into another's soul.

∞

Among the tribes of northern Natal in South Africa, the most common greeting—the equivalent of "hello" in English—is the expression *sawu bona*. Literally it means "I see you." If you are a member of the tribe you might reply by saying *sikhona,* which translates into English as "I am here." The order of the exchange is significant. It means that until you see me I do not exist; when you do see me, you bring me into existence. The meaning implicit in the perennial wisdom of these tribespeople is part of what is called *ubuntu,* a frame of mind or world-view characteristic of sub-Sahara African peoples. *Ubuntu* is the key word used to shorten a phrase in the Zulu language that translates "a person is a person because of other people."[1]

This ancient understanding squares with the contemporary wisdom of servant leadership. It is anchored in the empowering simplicity of "I see you," and the answering simplicity of "I am here" means that my personhood has been called into existence, along with all my gifts and potential. This does not mean that all the problems and stresses of leadership evaporate once the leader begins to "see." In all of us there is something that does not want to be seen—either by others or by our own selves. Self-protection operates as a barrier in all human interaction. But the "I see you" of servant leadership activates the mystical power of love and begins the process of release, in both the leader and the led, from the fears that inhibit the exchange of truth and drain the energy of collaboration. Most of all, a servant style of leadership reduces the leader's need to dominate. Responsi-

---

1. Peter M. Senge, *The Fifth Discipline Field Book* (New York: Doubleday, 1994), 3-4.

bility for the performance of others in any system or organization acts as an impatient inner urge to use our power to compel compliance, whether we are a frustrated mother who is tempted to force oatmeal on a stubborn child at breakfast or an overworked bishop who would like nothing better than to expel an incompetent parish priest whose congregation is suffocating.

This was certainly my problem during my years as a bishop. The Episcopal Church is a democratized version of the Church of England: the principal power is vested in the people and their parish clergy, not in the bishop. The bishop's domain is a geographic region called a diocese, but his or her power to lead is hedged about with sharp limits. A bishop in the Episcopal Church bears ultimate responsibility for the performance of parish clergy, but no clear authority either to deploy or to dismiss. In actual practice the bishop's role varies from diocese to diocese, depending on local tradition and the bishop's personal style, but on the whole he or she must rely on the power of persuasion and example, not on control.

Before election as a bishop I had been a parish priest and seminary teacher, but neither of these roles had prepared me for the lonely dynamics of a top-of-the-system job that often seemed more ornamental than functional. Furthermore, this structure of authority carries a large potential for frustration. I knew intuitively that the wisdom of an "I see you" approach to my clergy was the truly effective way; appeals to strength rather than condemnation of weakness accomplish much more because they arise from true appreciation. But how could I sharpen my intuition into an operating principle? How to fashion a vagrant idea into a leadership tool?

∞

It was then that I encountered the work of Robert Greenleaf through his essay *The Servant as Leader*. His words gave a voice to my intuition. I remember reading his essay while sitting at my desk one morning in the diocesan office. It was like locating a firm navigational fix from the stars at dusk. The essay was both a point of departure and a course to take into every tomorrow.

Greenleaf himself had been a senior executive in the old monolithic AT&T. On his retirement he had begun to write reflections on his learning about managing people over many years. The essay I read had been inspired by Herman Hesse's story of Leo, a humble servant to a pilgrim band on a *Journey to the East*. In Hesse's story all goes well for the pilgrims until circumstances deprive them of Leo, whose absence creates a vacuum of confusion and aimlessness. Eventually, without the leadership of this "servant," the pilgrimage has to be abandoned. Years later one of the pilgrims discovers that Leo is in fact the prior of a distinguished monastic community, the number one leader in a large arrangement of interlocking lives.

From that story Robert Greenleaf drew the insight that a truly effective leader is always servant *first*:

> He is sharply different from the person who is leader first.... The difference manifests itself in the care taken by the servant-first to make sure that other people's highest priority needs are being served.[2]

---

2. Robert K. Greenleaf, *The Servant as Leader* (Indianapolis: The Robert K. Greenleaf Center, 1991), 7.

This approach turned a piece of old scriptural piety into bold contemporary truth for me. No longer did I need to be intimidated by the two-fisted management habits and long-standing power structures of secular hierarchies, for Greenleaf taught me these habits were outmoded and counterproductive in any organization, profit and nonprofit alike. He gave me the heart to pitch out my envy for leaders of business organizations who, it appeared, could hire and fire and order people around at will. His wisdom squared with the wisdom of Jesus, who taught and lived the concept of servant leadership nearly two thousand years before. The prophet of Nazareth, faced with his followers' natural ambition for the conventional power of dominance, repudiated it:

> You know that among the Gentiles those whom they recognize as their rulers lord it over them, and their great ones are tyrants over them. But it is not so among you; but whoever wishes to become great among you must be your servant, and whoever wishes to be first among you must be slave of all. For the Son of Man came not to be served but to serve, and to give his life a ransom for many. (Mark 10:42-45)

My eyes were opened to see the piercing truth of this paradox. *The paradox is true not because Jesus said it. Jesus said it because it is true.* When Jesus reveals the formula for greatness in leadership he is not talking to a Sunday school class or propounding a truth that applies to some situation and not others. Instead, Jesus is teaching the truth of God's cosmos. He is the revealer of what is true in all settings, at all times, in all relationships. Servanthood is the path of greatness in marriage, in the marketplace, in government, and at General Motors. *Jesus reveals a way of life, not simply a way of being religious.*

Slowly it dawned on me that the frustration I was feeling at being denied the privilege of "lordship" as a bishop was the wisdom of a power structure that insists on the divine truth of mutuality. The system over which an Episcopal bishop or church leader presides is structured for a servant style of leadership.

This is not to say that servant structures of church governance cannot be abused, or that hierarchy is inherently oppressive. In history there are just kings and tyrannical kings, humble bishops and arrogant bishops, serving presidents and self-serving presidents—all with uneven mixtures of the good and the bad. It is not so much the system that shapes the character of leadership as the competing energies of love and fear in the heart of the leader. All leaders know the fear that leadership responsibilities arouse, and, when we are alert to the truth, we also know that fear arouses in turn the need to dominate and control. And if we have lived long enough we also know the pain of being resisted and rebuked by free souls who refuse to be abused—whether the system is structured in favor of hierarchy or worker participation.

In the long run, no leader is privileged to "lord it over" anyone, in any system, because the universe itself is constructed to honor the freedom of the human spirit. Systems that violate such freedom are doomed to topple in the revolt of subjugated children, oppressed employees, and tyrannized citizens, however long it takes. This is why servant leadership is foundational. Like a rock on which to anchor a house, it will secure any structure of human enterprise built upon it—families, businesses, churches, nations—as well as the emerging network of nations in their interlocking need of one another for the peace and protection of the planet.

This, then, is the work of the servant leader as I now define it: *to honor the personal dignity and worth of all who are led, and to evoke as much as possible their own innate creative power for leadership.* As I look back on my years of decision-making, I recall unilateral actions on my part that aroused needless conflict, whereas having the patience to listen to others and to be guided accordingly almost always led to wiser and happier outcomes. This did not mean avoiding controversy in large public issues, for I ardently supported the civil rights movement and strongly opposed the Vietnam war. In the latter case I publicly challenged Billy Graham to use his influence with President Nixon to halt the bombing. The winds of conflict blew hard, in the Atlanta press and throughout the churches. But even so, I believe that many more souls were girded than gored.

Leadership means going out ahead, and servanthood can mean risking the vilification of those who are offended by a leader's positions on controversial matters. But usually the offended ones are a strident minority. My experience is that the majority will be stretched and strengthened when the truth can be seen as serving the personal dignity and worth of all who are led.

When I finished reading Robert Greenleaf's stirring essay, I tracked him down through his publisher and invited him to share his convictions with me and my clergy, the ordained leadership of the Diocese of Atlanta. He spent a whole day with us, talking and listening. The substance of what he said was that a servant leader concentrates on building up the people, not on polishing the system or the leader's self-importance. When this is done, he said, the system will essentially build itself. Here he was ahead of the curve of research in physics. We are beginning to learn that systems actually *want* to build themselves because we live in what frontier science now calls "a self-organizing universe."[3] What this

---

3. See Erich Jantsch, *The Self-Organizing Universe* (Oxford: Pregamon Press, 1980).

comes down to is that servant leadership serves not only people but also the very thrust of life in the cosmos. Deep at the heart of things is both the longing and the energy to live. This explains why servanthood will almost always win a following, eventually. Those who are so led have been included as participants in the power of life, and even initial resisters and objectors can later experience the buoyancy that comes of having done it themselves.

In the years following that clergy conference Robert Greenleaf and I became friends and correspondents. At the invitation of Emory University, he and I became members of an educational design group in 1982. Our purpose was to create an experimental partnership between the distant disciplines of theology and management. We gave the experiment a name, not knowing whether or for how long it might be useful: the Institute for Servant Leadership. Through it we hoped that business and the church could each learn to function as institutional servants in the social order, maturing together in a world crying out for an infusion of moral courage and spiritual vigor. We believed that it was not necessary for institutions and systems to be spiritually oppressive and physically draining. We were driven by the conviction that institutions could be, in Greenleaf's words, *"enlargers and liberators of their people."*

For business, we hoped for a high sense of purpose that could turn bottom-line, short-term, exploitative goals into the promise of a more personally involving and fulfilling experience for the entire workforce, with a greater sensitivity to the public good on the part of owners, managers, and stockholders. For the church, we held up the vision of livelier worship and more inclusive decision-making. We hoped for leaders who would see their churches as centers of steady life-changing prayer, constant learning, and daring dispatch. We hoped for clergy who would see themselves as servants for developing and deploying Christian people with a keen sense of God's care for the world, along with the courage to challenge greed and injustice and to work for peace.

Today our society is in the midst of a turbulent transition from a world of competitive power structures to one of community and collaboration. The industrial era is dying, painfully and stubbornly. It is giving way to something we now only dimly see and find hard to name, but it will be an era tuned to a world that has become too small for violence and too precious for plunder. Servant leadership can guide and energize this transition, because it speaks to the deepest sensitivities of the human spirit. We see this transformative power in great servant leaders of the world as well as in the quiet seekers and practitioners of truth and love in kitchens, shops, and classrooms everywhere.

Servant leadership defines success as giving, and measures achievement by devotion to serving. Winning becomes the creation of community through collaboration, rather than the conquest of others by competition or crushing military superiority. In terms of servant leadership, being a "superpower" means using the nation's material, military, and spiritual wealth to help fulfill the longing of all people for a secure and healthy place in which to live.

The more I ponder its meaning, the more it reveals itself as an expression of comprehensive spiritual power. Servant leadership not only embodies the secret of the most creative human relationships, it also defines what I now believe to be the very character of God. Insofar as this is true, servant leadership suggests the need for a fresh metaphor in thinking about God, one that may startle those of us who are accustomed to thinking of God in terms of kingship—as dwelling on high, enthroned in the heavens. Servanthood is an image that is far more congruent with the revelation of God in the person of Jesus, as we shall see in the following chapter.

Years ago Justice Oliver Wendell Holmes said, "I wouldn't give a fig for simplicity this side of complexity, but I would give my life for simplicity on the other side of complexity." This longed-for simplicity on the other side of complexity reveals itself in care for one another and for the earth, and is the whole thrust of servant leadership. Grounded in love of the "Servant God" as the power that spins the stars, servant leadership is a life-giving simplicity *within* the world's complexity.

Chapter 2

The Paradox of Servant Leadership

We have seen what Jesus was like. If we wish now to treat him as our God, we would have to conclude that our God does not want to be served by us, he wants to serve.

—Albert Nolan

The idea of paradox in the abstract is murky, but in a *person* it can shine like moonlight on tranquil water. Paradox will always need incarnation—embodiment—in order to be real. Logic falls short as a persuader.

Consider the paradox of servant leadership. A servant is one who stands below and behind, while a leader's position is above and ahead. Logically then, it is impossible to make these two positions fit a single point in space or in the make-up of one person. But paradox, like servant leadership, is not bounded by logic. When paradox is understood as a formula for great truth, then the opposite of a great truth becomes another great truth. Servant and leader combine to form an ideal blend of personal attributes in *toughness* and *tenderness*.

These qualities sparkle like diamonds in the character of Jesus of Nazareth. His toughness comes through in his fearless rebuke of the religious establishment and his repeated assault on the hypocrisy of the conventionally religious. Jesus reached out in limitless care for the least and the lost—as well as to the privileged, as in the case of Nicodemus, a member of the ruling religious class. Jesus stands as the prototype of the servant leader. His moral demands take us to the highest possible ground, as in his call to love our enemies, and yet his mercy is boundless, as in his prayer of forgiveness for his executioners.

∞

The Christian theological tradition, from its earliest formulations, has held Jesus to be the incarnation of God: the life of God in human form. It is clear from the early gospels of Matthew, Mark, and Luke that Jesus identified himself not as a king, emperor, or ruler of any kind, but as a servant. In the gospel of John, written later than these, Jesus acts out the meaning of this identity in the astonishing gesture of washing the feet of his followers. Peter is abashed, at first curtly refusing to be so meanly served by his Lord, totally unprepared to understand messiahship as servanthood.

Yet servanthood is the biblical key to God's identity. Jesus, born in the starkest simplicity, went about the servant work of teaching, healing, and feeding, with eager compassion for the socially marginalized of his culture: the women, the children, the poor, the dying, and the dead. Repeatedly he risked the wrath of powerful religious authorities by rebuking the moral and social pretensions of the self-important. The servanthood of God was as implausible to those who knew Jesus best as it is to us—and yet it must be true. In John's gospel, the disciple Philip pleads with Jesus, "Lord, show us the

Father, and we will be satisfied." Jesus responds to him with a question: "Have I been with you all this time, Philip, and you still do not know me? Whoever has seen me has seen the Father" (John 14:8-9). Millions of devout believers have been steeped in a long tradition of prayer and hymnody in which God's power is pictured as unilateral dominance from on high. But the key New Testament images of God's presence as a living person are at sharp odds with this convention. As Jesus repaints the picture, the universe is the creation and dominion of the Servant God.

We cannot have it both ways. We cannot have a God who is an iron-handed ruler in remote control of the cosmos and, at the same time, a historic incarnation of that God who consistently defines himself as a servant. To those whom he most carefully instructed Jesus posed a question: "For who is greater, the one who is at the table or the one who serves? Is it not the one at the table? But I am among you as one who serves" (Luke 22:27). Such passages force us to choose between a God enthroned in the power of imperial privilege and a God "disenthroned" in the more exquisite power of servanthood—unless Jesus is not really God's self-disclosure. If the Christian doctrine of God is to be consistent with the orthodox claim that Jesus is God's incarnation, then the cosmos is ruled by a self-giving Love who chooses to endure crucifixion rather than decree any abridgment of human freedom.

As breathtaking as that act of divine love is, guarding human freedom at the cost of its very life, there is something even more significant in the action. The greater meaning lies in the disclosure of the Servant God whose self-giving love acts out a quantum advance in moral revelation—one that leaps far beyond the avenging ethic of "an eye for an eye" and forgives the very perpetrators of cosmic injustice. This is an advance of moral truth that humanity can still scarcely comprehend, let alone put into practice.

The crucifixion of the Servant God, who embraces the crucifiers in forgiving compassion, is foretold in a startling admonition in the Sermon on the Mount. There Jesus contrasts an older ethic with something utterly new and different in revealing the character of divine servanthood:

> You have heard that it was said, "You shall love your neighbors and hate your enemy." But I say to you, Love your enemies and pray for those who persecute you, so that you may be children of your Father in heaven. (Matthew 5:43-45)

What Jesus teaches, Jesus does! And he does it to the extremity of self-giving in suffering servanthood. This offering of self is at the heart of his power to be a leader, and is the key to both his identity as the messiah and his role as a servant leader who would challenge and transform the world.

"Leader" is a word for a person's role; "servant" can be a word for a person's identity. Role and identity are overlapping but very different components in everybody's personal make-up. They blend but cannot be confused without a loss of personal effectiveness. That is to say, one's role is not one's essence. Whether a parent or a president, anyone who makes decisions is a human being. The more one's real humanity as a leader comes through, whether in the home or in the Oval Office, the greater the chance that directness and compassion will be qualities that shine in all the people who make up that leader's system. Whether the system is a family or a business enterprise or a parish church, a leader's personal integrity will be reflected at all levels of responsibility. Every institution is the lengthened shadow of its principal leader, a shadow enriched and extended by the leadership of those who are led.

Decision-makers in every walk of life make mistakes. Leaders who are able to own their mistakes are the ones who engender the integrity and collaboration that are hallmarks of healthy families and vigorous systems. But keeping the distinction clear between role and identity is difficult work. There are at least two reasons for the difficulty.

The first reason is an emotional one. Pride and insecurity are bedeviling energies. Our drive and our ability tend to seduce us into thinking of ourselves as defined by the job we do: I am the father (commander) of this family; I am the president (in control) of this company; I am the rector (ruler) of this parish; I am the professor (biggest brain) in this class-room. The servant leader, by contrast, thinks: I am the fellow-human whose *responsibility* it is to love and guide this family, to serve and lead this parish, to point the direction for this company, to stimulate the learning process in this class-room.

When the lead persons in any enterprise habitually confuse role and identity, losing sight of the common humanity they share with the people they lead, an artificial distance is opened between the leaders and the led, and everybody suffers—nobody more than the leaders themselves. Pomposity in a leader encourages phoniness and posturing all through an organization. Self-importance cuts off the leader from the people at all levels, and it sabotages the caring and truthful relationships that can energize family units and whole systems.

Nowhere is this destructive energy more apparent than in familial relationships marked by abuse, whether parental or spousal. What we see in nearly every case of abuse is not power but impotence—the impotence of those whose sense of self is so weak that self-esteem must be sought in a perverse use of physical or intellectual or emotional superiority. In organizations where aggressive competition suppresses collaboration, there is apt to be a leader who carries a large burden of self-doubt and whose diminished sense of self needs boosting by pitting people against one another. In such systems blaming displaces personal responsibility, secrets multiply, and distrust robs work of its intrinsic joy.

Where the leader's self-appreciation is easy and strong, however, that person's leadership can be seen offering unbidden appreciation of others. A sturdy sense of personal identity in a leader does two kinds of work: it both *cheers* and *disciplines* a family or an enterprise. The spiritual result of such leadership is that an institution so led "enlarges and liberates its people," in Robert Greenleaf's definition of an institution at its best.

As a young naval line officer in World War II I sailed on two destroyers. The first was commanded by a tall and impressive Harvard graduate; the skipper of the second ship stood five feet five and had no educational credentials beyond the naval academy. Life on board the first vessel was a constant guessing game about the captain's mood swings; he reminds me now of the deeply insecure Captain Queeg in *The Caine Mutiny*. But life had a lilt under my second skipper, whose ship was a sea-going castle of quality. What the captain lacked in physical stature he more than made up for in spirit, a towering presence of cheerful and decisive command. It was a matter of pride to be attached to the USS Caperton DD 650 of the Pacific fleet in the mid 1940s.

The second reason for the difficulty in separating role and identity lies in the challenge of paradox. Servant leadership itself is a paradox that looks like a rational absurdity, an oxymoron, a contradiction. Actually, it is the dynamic relationship of two apparently opposing truths that require one another to be wholly true, like the twin necessities of rigorous law and forgiving love that make life with others socially possible. Paradox is thus a formula for the *whole* truth. The great difficulty with paradox is that the two opposing truths which make a whole truth also make a teeter-totter—an unsteady board on a bar, impossible to hold in perfect balance. Paradox is like a destroyer's uneven roll from port to starboard when steaming through wind-blown waters.

The blend of servanthood and leadership is a paradox that marks many of the truly great people of history. Carl Sandburg tells a true story about Abraham Lincoln that paints a vivid picture of the essential paradox of servant leadership. During the Civil War President Lincoln was visited by a Colonel Scott, one of the commanders of troops guarding the capital from attack by Confederate forces in Northern Virginia. Scott's wife had died, drowned in a steamboat collision in Chesapeake Bay when returning home after a journey to Washington to nurse her sick husband. Scott had appealed to regimental command for leave to attend her burial and comfort his children. His request had been denied; a battle seemed imminent and every officer was essential. But Colonel Scott, as was his right, had pressed his request up the chain of command until it had reached the Secretary of War, Edwin Stanton. Since Stanton had also denied the request, the colonel had taken his appeal all the way to the top.

Scott got to his commander-in-chief in the presidential office late on a Saturday night, the last visitor allowed in. Lincoln listened to the story and, as Scott recalled his response, the President exploded: "Am I to have no rest? Is there no hour or spot when or where I may escape these constant calls? Why do you follow me here with such business as this? Why do you not go to the War Office where they have charge of all this matter of papers and transportation?"

Scott told Lincoln of Stanton's refusal, and the President replied, "Then you probably ought not to go down the river. Mr. Stanton knows all about the necessities of the hour; he knows what rules are necessary, and rules are made to be enforced. It would be wrong of me to override his rules and decisions of this kind; it might work disaster to important movements. And then, you ought to remember that I have other duties to attend to—heaven knows, enough for one man—and I can give no thought to questions of this kind. Why do you come here to appeal to my humanity? Don't you know that we are in the midst of war? That suffering and death press upon all of us? That works of humanity and affection, which we would cheerfully perform in days of peace, are all trampled upon and outlawed by war? That there is no room left for them? There is but one duty now—to fight!...Every family in the land is crushed with sorrow; but they must not each come to me for help. I have all the burdens I can carry. Go to the War Department. Your business belongs there. If they cannot help you, then bear your burden, as we all must, until this war is over. Everything must yield to the paramount duty of finishing this war."

Colonel Scott returned to his barrack, brooding. Early the next morning he heard a rap at the door. He opened it and there stood the President. He took Scott's hands, held them, and broke out: "My dear Colonel, I was a brute last night. I have no excuse to offer. I was weary to the last extent, but I had no right to treat a man with rudeness who has offered his life to his country, much more a man in great affliction. I have had a regretful night, and come now to beg your forgiveness." He said he had arranged with Stanton for Scott to go to his wife's burial. In his own carriage the commander-in-chief took the colonel to the steamer wharf on the Potomac and wished him Godspeed.[1]

Servanthood and leadership blend as a paradox that marks the great people of history. This is not to say, however, that servant leadership is a state of human perfection unapproachable for most of us. It is an ideal toward which to strive and a quality of character to cultivate and attain, but decidedly *not* an impossible peak to scale. Greatness of humanity is always among us. If a group of people is asked to name those who have been servant leaders for them the lists grow quickly. Their servant leaders will be parents, teachers, grandparents, coaches, priests and pastors, sisters and brothers. Servant leaders are those whose lives affect the lives of others for good: doctors, chambermaids, executives, teachers, mechanics, merchants, maybe even a politician now and then like Lincoln or the Kennedys of our time. All of them will have flaws. Personal imperfections never disqualify an aspirant to servant leadership. Too many great ones, for all their accomplishments and strength of character, are flawed at critical points—and admit it. Mohandas Gandhi openly owned his failure as a father. His oldest son, a moral disaster, nursed his alienation from the family for years. Abraham Lincoln acknowledged his deep regret at his callous impatience with one of his soldiers suffering with grief. The blemishes in heroes are signs of the profoundest paradox of servant leadership: *perfection lies precisely in the readiness to own one's imperfection.*

At the age of seventy-two Carl Sandburg wrote a preface for a volume of his collected poems. He closed the piece with

---

1. Carl Sandburg, *Lincoln: The War Years* (New York: Scribner and Sons, 1939), 513-514.

a few stirring sentences that I have cherished for years, because they are Sandburg's own disavowal of perfection.

> All my life I have been trying to learn to read, to see and
> hear, and to write....I should like to think that as I go on
> writing there will be sentences truly alive, with verbs
> quivering, with nouns giving color and echoes. It could
> be that I shall live to be eighty-nine, as did Hokousai, and
> speaking my farewell to earthly scenes, I might para-
> phrase: "If God had let me live five years longer I should
> have been a writer."[2]

Anyone who writes has got to be a bit daft. Not only is it
arduous work, this mining from deep inside one's self, but it
is also a constant warfare between the forces of perfectionism and hard reality. You want your work to be imperishably
vivid and polished, but you know that you are never going to
get the work beyond moderate improvement. You lack the
ingenuity to perfect your writing beyond even your own
critique, let alone beyond the critical scrutiny of editors and
readers.

Annie Dillard knows the truth of this elusive perfection.
As a distinguished servant leader of letters she has crafted a
penetrating essay about the church's failure to be a community of the perfected. Writing of the final verses of Luke's
gospel, which tell of the skies closing around the ascending
soles of Jesus' feet, followed by his disciples' flurry of activity
in the temple, Dillard says,

> What a pity that so hard on the heels of Christ come the
> Christians. There is no breather. The disciples turn into
> the early Christians between one verse and another. What

---

2. Carl Sandburg, *Harvest Poems* (New York: Harcourt Brace
Jovanovich, 1960), 14-15.

a dismaying pity, that here come the Christians already—
flawed to the core, full of wild ideas and hurried self-importance. They are already blocking, with linked arms,
the howling gap in the weft of things that their man's
coming and going tore.[3]

Dillard describes the paradox of a perfection that is free
to embrace its own imperfection. Jesus is the prototype of the
servant leader, and he invited into his ranks the brazenly
imperfect people called to join him in servanthood. What
this means is that God is not a perfectionist. God cannot be
a perfectionist and continue to allow the world to exist,
especially that part of the world that follows Jesus and yet
looks so little like him—the church. Many of us who know
the church intimately regard her as a living creature, born of
the merciful work of God and tended by the awkward stewardship of the flawed and forgiven. We are often disap-
pointed by this old institution and disenchanted with its
leadership, and yet it is possible to give the creature an
honest love, knowing that our own sins are part of the great
deposit of imperfection which God has embraced from the
beginning. Loving the church is akin to what Shakespeare's
Falstaff says about his horse, "She is a sorry beast, but she is
mine own." The church is a treasured old beast, knock-kneed
and sway-back, yet ever renewed by the grace of God and the
flawed fidelity of good people.

God cannot be a perfectionist and still keep loving arms
around the church and the world. The non-perfectionism of
the perfect God is the deepest layer of revealed truth in the
Christian tradition, the silk source and iron mine from which

---

3. Annie Dillard, an essay on the Acts of the Apostles in *Incarnation:
   Contemporary Writers on the New Testament*, Alfred Corn, ed.
   (Baltimore: Penguin, 1990), 36.

the velvet and steel of servant leadership is fashioned. But, it might be asked, does this not contradict the admonition of Jesus that has bedeviled generations of Christians burdened by the perfectionist impulse? He laid on his followers a requirement that seems to give divine sanction to the merciless demands we lay on ourselves: "Be perfect, therefore, as your heavenly Father is perfect" (Matthew 5:48). Notice, however, that his command to be perfect is mercifully qualified. The standard for Jesus is not human but divine, not legal but gracious: *"as your heavenly Father is perfect."* Understanding this qualification is like getting out of jail. It releases one from the oppression of human perfectionism because it measures perfection by the standard of an invincible mercy: "as your heavenly Father is perfect." God's perfectionism is anti-perfectionist.

Herein lies the breathtaking freedom of servant leaders, their foundational paradox. The power and perfection of servanthood lies precisely in the embrace of imperfection. I believe this is what St. Paul had in mind when he dashed off that marvelously liberating sentence: "There is therefore now no condemnation for those who are in Christ Jesus" (Romans 8:1). "Grace"—the unmerited mercy of God—is the word for this release from reprobation, this freedom from the punitive demands of perfectionism.

Perfectionism is not mature enough to enjoy life. Perfectionism is nervously adolescent, driven by fear of failure, dominated by the competitive pride that would rather save oneself than accept the amazing grace "that saves a wretch like me." Knowing deep down that our perfectionism fails, we hide from our own flaws behind the failures of others, habitually confessing other people's sins. Carl Jung called this adolescent maneuver "projecting our own shadow": the perverse and popular talent for seeing vividly in others the darkness we cannot bear to behold in ourselves, which makes battlefields of families and organizations. Projection, said Jung, is the core source of war.

Servant leadership will always need the foundation of an embracing grace. The biggest hindrance to the high quality of leadership that honors the gifts and freedom of others is the fear of being found out for who we really are: people who are *conspicuously imperfect*. Every follower sees blameworthiness in every leader. And when leaders can see it too—see it even better than their followers—and own it from the mercy by which they are secured, then everything changes. The family, the business, the parish church become arenas of openness, honesty, caring, and collaboration. They are marked by grace and truth.

Any enterprise marked by the grace and truth of servant leadership has this principle of conspicuous imperfection incarnated in real persons at many levels of responsibility in the system—best of all, at the top. No principle can make an enterprise gracious. Only persons bring grace to institutions.

Chapter 3

Power and the Servant Leader

The capacity to absorb an influence is as truly a mark of power as is the strength involved in exerting an influence.

—Bernard Loomer

On Palm Sunday, April 9, 1865, just down the road from a small house in Appomattox, Virginia, Robert E. Lee rode his horse Traveler between two rows of exhausted soldiers. The tattered and hungry men had been camped disconsolately in clusters along a dusty trail. They awaited what they knew would be the surrender of the army in which they had served and suffered, some of them from the first engagement at Bull Run four years before. The general was returning to his tent, about a mile to the rear, after a brief surrender ceremony with Ulysses S. Grant. As Lee appeared in solemn dignity a rush of troops rose to greet him, two solid walls of gaunt men standing along the whole distance. As he entered the avenue of soldiers wild cheers broke the stillness. Unprepared for this tribute in defeat, the general's composure slackened and tears started down his cheeks. Seeing their leader's emotion, the soldiers' shouts gradually turned to choking sobs. Each segment of troops in the mile-long corridor began and ended their response the same way, first with cheers and then with muted cries. At the very end of the line a grizzled sergeant reached out his hand and, touching the now empty scabbard at his captain's side, said through his tears, "I love you just as well as ever, General Lee."[1]

At its base servant leadership is an attribute of the soul, a spiritual gift, like integrity or compassion. Servant leadership, like any innermost quality, is easier to define as what it is *not* than what it *is*. Someone described integrity as something you cannot see until it is not there, and servanthood is the same. It is neither dominance nor servility. Instead, it is the most enduring form of power, because it is congruent with the relational way things work in the ongoing life of the universe. We know from the quantum insights of postmodern science that everything in creation interconnects. The totality of the created order is a kind of hidden but immensely real network of interrelation. Thus it is that the successful exercise of power, one that achieves the goal of the exerciser, will strive to honor the network of interdependence within which power is exercised.

Conventional leadership varies widely, but all varieties bear a common stamp: they use power to control people and to limit the range of individual differences. Such a concept of power is both illusory and counterproductive—illusory because humanity is built for freedom, counterproductive because when power is understood as control, the more it is applied the more it is resisted. Resistance to the use of power as control springs directly from the first proposition, namely that the human soul is made for freedom. Again, true power is always an exchange of power. This is true even when

---

1. Douglas Southall Freeman, *Robert E. Lee* (New York: Scribner and Sons, 1935-1936), vol. 4, 146-47.

subordinates appear powerless. It took seventy-four years to overthrow the Soviet communism of Eastern Europe, but the power of the powerless eventually delegitimized a vast tyranny, and communist control was dismantled in a week. Earlier in history, in the case of the mutiny on April 28, 1789 against the tyranny of Captain William Bligh of HMS *Bounty,* the dismantling of oppressive power took far less time, maybe seventy-four days, but it was bound to come. The character of God's reality determines the disastrous outcome of tyranny.

Such consequences need not be convulsive and bitter. Resistance to the tyranny of manipulation and coercion can engender happy consequences. When resistance to tyranny issues in positive results the key to this kind of outcome lies in the soul of the leader. Not all coercive leaders are unable to ease up on their coercion. Not all tyrants are resistant to a change of heart; not all are Queegs or Blighs.

Picture the climactic scene in L. Frank Baum's great American myth, *The Wizard of Oz.* Four supplicants stand nervously in the throne room of the Great Oz: Dorothy with her small dog Toto, the Tin Woodsman, the Scarecrow, and the Cowardly Lion. All but the dog are hoping for a gift from the Wizard. Dorothy wants to get home to Kansas; the Tin Woodsman wants a heart; the Scarecrow wants a brain; the Lion wants his roar. Trembling, they stand before a great wall marked by the apparition of an oversized and dimly discernible human face veiled by clouds of steam. The face speaks. The voice is *basso-profundo,* as if emanating from a cave, every other word accompanied by a fresh burst of menacing steam. All the supplicants are stupefied with dread—but not the dog. Toto trots to the side of the throne room, tugs at a curtain, and behold! There stands an ordinary man at an electronic console, talking into a microphone and manipulating levers.

Dorothy is the first of the four to react. She recovers her composure, strides over to the console, stamps her foot, and shouts an accusing rebuke: "Oh, you are a bad man!" The Wizard, embarrassed but speaking his own truth, replies, "No, no—I am a good man, just a bad wizard!"

The important lesson for leadership here is that real power rises from authenticity, not from appearances or manipulation. Real leadership is never wizardry. It always springs from unpretentious humanity. What this means is that an easy humanness is the foundation of servanthood, and that servanthood is the chief modifier of the power implicit in all leadership—a quality of innerness, an attribute of soul that checks the corruptibility of power. Lord Acton's terse warning is important: "Power corrupts; absolute power corrupts absolutely." But it need not be so. Servanthood is the corrective, and the Wizard was effective in his use of power only when the *truth* of his humanity was declared and embraced.

Pretense is lying about reality. Lies are bitter seeds in the soil of life, germinating as alienation, distance, and distrust. Pretense leads to the reduction of the power to lead, not its enhancement—for everyone from parents to presidents. The tragedy of Richard Nixon is the public case in point. His deceit destroyed him as a leader and continues to obscure his remarkable accomplishments. In the six years of his presidency he was responsible for the creation of the Environmental Protection Agency and the Occupational Safety and Health Administration. He signed the Clean Air Act, indexed Social Security to the cost of living, quietly dismantled the segregated public-school systems of the South, and made affirmative action a central part of civil rights legislation. Wholesale ignorance of these achievements of Nixon's "progressive conservatism" underscore the ultimate consequence of concealing the truth, which is the death of effective leadership. We beheld this publicly when Nixon could never fully acknowledge the truth of his humanity.

This raises another question of concern to servant leaders. Why do people lie? Given our freedom to speak the truth, and given the fact that lying is so destructive, why is deceit so much a part of human behavior? The movie *Charade,* with Cary Grant and Audrey Hepburn, has a piece of dialogue that explains it well. As they are pursuing a thief Hepburn asks Grant, "Why do people lie?" He replies, "People lie because they want something and fear that the truth will not get it for them."

Fear is the operative emotion in all leadership that fails, chiefly fear to know and to be oneself. Pretense cancels out the only real authority anyone has. The power of inner oneness with God and keen self-knowledge were Jesus of Nazareth's only credentials. His detractors badgered him repeatedly with questions about his authority. They knew he had none, so they sought to discredit him on the basis of his lack of professional standing. Even his family found him an embarrassment, urging him to get hold of himself and come home with them (Mark 3:31).

In the Oz myth, the Wizard's truthfulness became a power not only for himself, but for others as well. All the supplicants got what they came for, not so much because the Wizard bestowed gifts, but because in his truthfulness he evoked what was already there. The symbol of this is Dorothy's awakening to what was true about her and Toto all along. The land of Oz was simply a dream precipitated by a tornado that blew Dorothy about in the family farmyard and knocked her unconscious. She had been in Kansas through it all, and, with the help of the Wizard become servant leader, she simply awakened to her real presence there.

∞

The ability to empower is what makes great leadership a servanthood: it awakens the slumbering power in the souls of others. I believe this is always the quiet work of the Holy Spirit, and the function of leadership is to awaken trust in the Spirit—to open people to the presence of the Holy Spirit within themselves and in one another. What this can accomplish is a surge of generosity that transforms situations of scarcity into festivals of plenty. It is at the root of every successful attempt at fundraising. Fundraising may be the most resisted of all the functions of church leadership and the most dreaded responsibility of church leaders, clergy and laity alike. But the girding truth is that the human soul is built to give. We are fashioned in the image of the Giver of all life, and nothing proves this more dramatically and repeatedly than the glow of fulfillment that accompanies every act of generosity. To challenge people to give is to do them a favor— the favor of acting out of their highest selves, made in the innermost pattern of the self-giving Servant God.

Why else are we so moved by the gleeful redemption of Ebenezer Scrooge on Christmas morning? That story has the power of the Spirit to exalt us year after year after year, and to move us to grasp again our joy as givers. Why else is the feeding of the multitude the single episode in the ministry of Jesus that was recorded in all four gospels? It is because these stories make vivid the truth that sharing turns apparent scarcity to rich abundance. The miracle work of Jesus on so many occasions is the evoking of gifts already present. Repeatedly he says of those in whom miracles of healing are experienced, "Your faith has made you well!" Your faith, not my wizardry. What is this but solid biblical evidence that the servanthood of Jesus functions over and again to call forth the waiting powers of health and holiness in ordinary people?

Real power is always an exchange of power. It is always the deep purpose of leadership to use power to call out the God-given power of others. As much as it may appear otherwise, the exercise of power is never a transaction between the powerful and the powerless. If it appears so it is because the apparently powerless are not exercising *their* power. Anita Roddick, founder of The Body Shop, paints a slogan on her trucks: "If You Ever Feel Too Small to Make a Difference, Try Getting in Bed with a Mosquito."

Since true power is an exchange of power, it will always be resisted when it is applied as unilateral control, whether it is the boss demanding conformity or the rector taking charge or the bishop attempting to intimidate. The more this kind of control is resisted, the more it raises frustration in the one who controls and therefore leads to redoubled attempts at control. Thus the energy flow in control systems tends to tighten the bands of resistance among those who are led and, at the same time, to weaken the bonds of connection between leader and led.

By the design of its Maker, the human spirit is intended for freedom, a disciplined freedom within the bounds of allegiance and accountability. Nothing proves this truth more forcibly than the history of human slavery. What was accepted as a social norm in our sacred writings, as in St. Paul's letter to Philemon, has now become morally and legally inadmissible. Built as we are for freedom and allegiance, our resistance to control mounts as pressures to control increase. Increasing control reduces responsiveness and productivity, which in turn moves human feeling in two directions for all parties involved. Satisfaction moves down; alienation moves up. Control systems discourage friendship. They are marked by grudging compliance and high turnover.

Children tend to leave home early in controlling families and become controlling parents in turn.

At their worst, control systems are kept in place by violence, coercion, and threat. Since power systems of control almost always arise from fear, the fundamental anxiety could be a sense that the arena of human life is essentially unfriendly. Deep in our souls we all make choices about the character of the universe. Einstein said that the most important question we ask comes down to this: "Is the universe friendly?" Having grown up in a culture shaped to so-called scientific norms of what is true, it may be that most of us today operate as if the universe is either indifferent or governed by rules of moral stringency. A Sunday school boy was asked to tell what he thought about God. The boy pondered a moment and then said, frowning, "God is a big policeman who looks for people who are having fun and then puts a stop to it!"

If pressed to describe our daily operating theology, we might well say this: God is either absent, having given creation a good wind-up and then left it to run on its own, or God is lurking in the mists looking for lawbreakers. If God is absent, then humanity is alone in the universe. We are compelled to compete in an endless power struggle for personal approval and a limited supply of desirable goods. Jesus chided people for not trusting God. The most commonly repeated admonition in the teaching of Jesus is the simple *fear not.* "But if God so clothes the grass of the field, which is alive today and tomorrow is thrown into the oven, will he not much more clothe you—you of little faith? Therefore do not worry" (Matthew 6:30-31). If, on the other hand, God is ominously present, prowling the human scene in an unmarked patrol car, then power is truly as *Webster's Unabridged* defines it: "Dominance and control...the ability to compel obedience." Power thus understood means fundamentally "the control of human perversity."

Whether the universe is viewed as empty of God or under God's controlling scrutiny, either way power will be exercised out of fear. And the greater the fear the greater the amount of implicit and explicit violence. The result is fear-driven lives for both the powerless and the powerful—the powerless fearing discrimination, injustice, and oppression, the powerful fearing resistance, rebellion, and loss of profit or status.

If this analysis is true, then leadership is a spiritual issue. Whether we acknowledge it or not, our conviction about the character of the universe directly affects our personal use of power. Thus leadership, at its core, is a theological issue, a matter of human belief about God. To accept Jesus of Nazareth as the prototype of the servant leader is to embrace his belief about God: the universe is neither indifferent nor unfriendly. It is for us! God loves us better than we love ourselves. God does not reject us because we are short, jug-eared, old, paunchy, and slow with numbers. Nor are we loved because we are tall, slim, and intellectually robust. God laughs at all that as anxious nonsense. God is far older than anybody, and weighs more than the whole cosmos. God allowed flawed people write the Bible—and flawed people to decide what to include in sacred scripture and what to leave out. That God would trust the theological core of divine self-revelation to a high-handed rabbi like St. Paul means that God risks everybody else's freedom, too. God bets on our capacity to respond to love and to live lovingly, never violating our freedom to choose, ready at all times to receive us as we are, as we have been, as we will be.

Even God's laws are embracing boundaries of love—designed not for God's protection, but for ours. Better still, the commandments are permeable membranes, not prison walls. They are fences with gates that swing both ways. When we are out, we can get back in. This is the whole point of the parable of the prodigal son, probably the best-remembered story Jesus told. The young man forsook home and family to become a thankless vagabond with half his father's fortune and proceeded to break all the rules. But he returned a stricken penitent, *blaming no one but himself*, and was banqueted in forgiveness. The servant leader takes the risk of believing that the universe is not only alive with the presence of God, but vibrant with grace. God gives and forgives.

The principles of servant leadership outlined here—making room for others, truthfulness, empowerment, the exchange of power rather than control, a belief in grace and forgiveness—are appealing as ideals, but they are difficult to apply in human systems, for at least two reasons. The first reason is the pervasive fear already discussed. The second reason lies in the hierarchical patterns of control to which the human enterprise in the West have been habituated for at least five millennia. In spite of the miraculous birth of "government of the people, by the people, and for the people," we continue to fear too much freedom in the ranks because freedom risks outcomes that interfere with the production purposes of organizations. Coffee breaks, it is feared, will turn into picnics unless the workforce is policed—if you give people an inch, they will take a mile.

But a servant leader does not see production as the first purpose of an enterprise. *Human enhancement,* not human employment, is the primary aim of organizations led by servants. Delivering a product or service is important but secondary, in the same way that competition is inherent in human systems but secondary to collaboration. Meaning and joy in work, as in church and in family life, derive far more from collaborative relationships than from competitive achievement—from *power with* rather than *power over.* In terms of human nourishment, collaboration is the meat and potatoes; competition, at best, is only salt and pepper. Our devotion to competition means that a whole society has been subsisting on spices!

Even our educational processes are driven by the competitive impulse, assuming that grades are the grand motivator of performance and the measure of personal value. Conventional education in this country can scarcely be conceived apart from a competitive scoring system in the classroom, not even theological education. Not long ago a group of African students who had recently arrived at the Candler School of Theology of Emory University turned in a paper they had worked on jointly. When the professor inquired, "Whose paper is this?" they answered, "Ours." It blew the grading process galley-west and confused the record-keepers. No one had bothered to tell them that in America they were expected to work alone, as *competitors*, not as collaborators.

My earliest memory of a competitive reward system endures from second grade. The teacher, a woman of iron resolve, was a cunning child motivator. She divided the class into three groups: bluebirds, busybees, and fireflies. These were all happy-sounding words to disguise the real distinctions she had in mind. But there was no disguising the distinctions if you were cast in group three. If you were a firefly you were of minimal value—a classroom drag unless you could drag yourself to next level.

Chester Funk was a firefly. He may well have had a good mind, but his spirit was an empty bucket. He could not rise above the lowest rung on the ladder in spelling drills. There were other fireflies, of course, but Chester remains vivid in my memory as a tragic symbol of the demonic character of all institutions built on competition. They intimidate and devalue persons. They even devalue the winners, by insinuating that an individual must be better than others in order to have any value. This is a profoundly *subversive* lesson in life, for it cheats a child of doing things for the joy of doing them, and of using the energies and talents unique to each person. No wonder so many of us grow up fearful of not measuring up; no wonder we have to resort to therapy as a way of repudiating the lessons learned from competition.

My second-grade teacher is not altogether to blame; her purpose was to get us all to fly with the bluebirds, or at least to do better. But an inherent counterproductivity was built into her system. Because we were pitted against standards established and preserved by the lead group itself, the system made it impossible for all but a few of us to make it to the bluebird perch. Perhaps worst of all, it was a system that defined collaboration as cheating, tilting the whole enterprise in favor of only the most gifted achievers and discouraging us from learning to work together toward a common goal.

Only once did I soar with the bluebirds. In a memory drill I named all the capitals of the states without a flaw (there were only forty-eight then). For about two weeks I basked in the company of bluebirds like Lester Fellner and Rose Schaufmann. Lester was born with a computer under his scalp, and Rose could recite verses as if she had eaten them for breakfast. I do not recall what sent me down to the minors as a busybee again, but it had to be some failure to compete successfully—probably in arithmetic, having demonstrated all my life a stupefying sluggishness with numbers. Lots of us in the busybee hive (we were the largest group in the room) graduated from second grade convinced we did not measure up, our only consolation being that we did not have to stagger into third grade as fireflies.

It took years as a certified busybee for me to discover three things. First, self-worth has almost nothing to do with IQ. In later years I found friends who blew the top off the brains chart but who struggled far more than I did to appreciate themselves. Second, it was fear of failure, not inferior ability, that kept me in the minors. Who would not grow up either scared or arrogant (which is nothing but fear disguised as bombast) in a system that values only the built-in power of your brains—for which no one can rightly claim credit or assume blame? Third, the real engine of human endeavor is a genetically programmed preference for collaboration over competition. As the human species emerged, we began to collaborate in specialties like hunting and gathering, which in turn created societies, communities of mutual care.

Servant leaders know this pull toward collaboration intuitively. Collaborative systems are designed around such factors as *shared vision,* a keen sense of *belonging,* and the *courage to tell the truth* in all relationships. The reason that such collaboration lifts the spirit of human work is that it appeals to the *best* of who we are rather than the *basest* of our motives, encouraging the offering of everyone's personal gifts for doing and improving the work. Such systems enlarge and enhance the lives of their members. The secret lies in setting and sustaining the high purpose of goals of service that go beyond private satisfactions. This is true in all systems: families, business enterprises, churches, and nations in their domestic and global security. Systems fail when their leaders exploit their people and practice deceit. Systems succeed when their leaders cherish their people and speak the truth.

Servant leaders are tuned to this. But they face a constant struggle with the demonic forces in all institutions, the pervasive evil that uses people to satisfy a system's appetites for control. Insofar as servant leaders prevail in this neverending struggle with what the Bible calls "the principalities and powers," they will build families, schools, churches, businesses, and governments in which people are cherished by being included in the exercise of power.

Nothing could better the describe work of love, nor better define the purpose of the church. To be enlarged and liberated in the company of fellow-pilgrims is to experience what Christian theology has always called "salvation." It is accomplished by God in response to what Jesus called "repentance"—an act of human freedom that repeatedly chooses to tell the truth and to love God as one's commanding allegiance. Such allegiance reshapes the world and all its institutions by the power of truth and love lived out.

It is to the life of the church that we turn in Part II.

Part II

∞

Servant Leadership in the Church

Chapter 4

Jesus as Servant Leader

Since the time of the Apostles, the history of faith and theology has been concerned with the mystery of the crucified Jesus himself; and it has been a history of permanent revisions, reformations and revolts, aimed at recognizing him for the person he really is and conforming to him by changing one's own life and thinking.

—Jürgen Moltmann

By any measurement, Jesus of Nazareth is the historic embodiment of what this study means by "servant leader." The servant leader can be anyone, in any station, whose life and work touches the lives of others and influences the character of the world. More has been written about Jesus of Nazareth than about any person of history, and more has been written in the past twenty-five years than in the previous two thousand. Why so? I think that the chief reason for this heightened interest in history's most commanding figure lies in what I claimed at the beginning of this book: that the human odyssey is going through an unparalleled sea-change.

We ought not to be surprised at the religious ferment that accompanies this upheaval; history has been through it before, as when the medieval era gave way to the industrial age. Today both church and society worldwide convulse in the grip of a new reformation, and the person of Jesus commands new curiosity and concern both within the church and beyond it. While organized Christianity in the mainline churches is in decline, Jesus has always been bigger than the church that names him Savior and Lord. As theologian Albert Nolan writes:

> Jesus cannot be fully identified with that great religious phenomenon of the Western world known as Christianity. He was much more than the founder of one of the world's great religions. He stands above Christianity as the judge of all it has done in his name. Nor can historical Christianity claim him as its exclusive possession. Jesus belongs to all [humanity].[1]

The centerpiece this brief study is neither the Jesus of history nor the Christ of faith. It is both. It must be both, because these two dimensions of Jesus cannot be separated without a tacit denial that our knowledge of Jesus, both ancient and modern, is dependent on the indisputable fact that *the Jesus of history would be a cipher in the record of executed criminals were it not that those who first loved him remembered his historical life and understood who he was from the perspective of their continuing life with him after his death.*

Still, the Jesus of history and the Christ of faith, while inseparable to the *fact* of Christianity, can be explored separately as *eras* of Christian history. Thus in this book on servanthood, which is bound up in Jesus' life and death and

---

1. *Jesus Before Christianity* (Maryknoll, N.Y.: Orbis Books, 1976), 3.

continuing life, there is a chapter on the historical Jesus and another one on the post-Easter Christ. This chapter seeks an understanding of the "servant mandate" that forced a crucifixion; the chapter that follows examines the impact of his resurrection in creating the "servant church." But separating "servant mandate" from "servant church" does not cleave in two what should be kept whole. It makes crucifixion and resurrection the hub of the Christian phenomenon: the servant mandate leads up to crucifixion-resurrection and the servant church flows out from it.

Jesus is the crucified God. This means that any adequate understanding of Jesus and his vast and mounting impact on the world must try to get at the reason why the "best people in town," the heavy hitters in both church and state, would conspire to kill the "best who ever lived."

The answer is both simple and complex. It is simple in that Jesus profoundly offended the powerful—both their leadership and the structures that supported it. It is complex because the sources of his offense and threat lie so deep within us that their truth continues to offend and threaten the structures of both church and society. Therefore it is both easy and painful to follow Jesus. He is a hero to cherish as well as a revolutionary to avoid. He invites both discipleship and rejection. He did so during his life on earth, and he continues to do so through all of history since—down to this day. And nothing he is remembered to have said better explains this paradox of love and suffering in following Jesus than his invitation to be a follower:

> He called the crowd with his disciples, and said to them, "If any want to become my followers, let them deny themselves and take up their cross and follow me. For those who want to save their life will lose it, and those who lose

their life for my sake, and for the sake of the gospel, will
save it." (Mark 8:34-35)

Just as crucifixion and resurrection form the centerpiece of
the life and work of Jesus, so too the cross and its promise of
life reborn are central to his invitation to live. If we can
discover what he means by "for the sake of the gospel" we
will also understand the "why" of both his crucifixion and his
continuing impact on the world. The reason that the gospel
is the clue to his life and death and continuing life is that his
proclamation of the truth about God, and our relationship to
God, was sharply at odds with the prevailing religious and
social norms. It was, and continues to be, revolutionary.

The revolutionary quality of his "gospel truth" is exactly
what makes Jesus the prototype of the servant leader in
history, and explains why servant leadership is itself a revolutionary concept. Its central impulse is its insistence on
"inclusion," its boundary-shattering energy of love that ex-
cludes no one in the whole human family and, by implica-
tion, not even the smallest pulse and particle of life in God's
cosmos. Small wonder that Robert Greenleaf said to me years
ago that servant leadership is a concept "mildly applauded
and much resisted—even in the churches, where it is as little
practiced as in the most competitive and dictatorial business
system." That assessment is now two decades old. Were he
alive today I believe he would take heart, as I do, in beholding
how much servanthood has gained acceptance—both as
ideology and practice, in business circles especially. Still, the
revolutionary Jesus is an offense to convention.

Consider the boundary-shattering impulse of the gospel
for which Jesus gave up his life. This revolutionary impulse
has two main features that I want to focus on: its universal
grace and its power to forgive. The term "grace" in the New
Testament, especially in the writings of Paul, means the free

unmerited love and forgiveness of God. In this definition the key word that distinguishes Jesus as a revolutionary is "unmerited." Understood against the background of the prevailing Jewish code of behavior by which one was regarded as either "righteous" or "unrighteous," an unmerited status of righteousness was unthinkable. That is to say, the primary way of righteousness for the Jew of Jesus' time was obedience to the strict provisions of the law—the law of Moses and the elaborations of the law that defined and governed good Jewish behavior.

The idea of righteousness bestowed freely and wholesale to all as an unmerited gift was a disruptive scandal, for it challenged many assumptions of Jewish religious thought and appeared to take lightly the requirements of the covenant. The pivotal declaration of Jesus in his gospel, both in his words and deeds, was precisely the scandal that *righteousness is a gift from the heart of a compassionate God.* This may have been why Jesus was charged by the Jerusalem establishment with being a "blasphemer against God," the charge at the heart of the accusations that prompted his trial before the high Jewish Council, the Sanhedrin. It was also the charge that set him before Pilate, who reluctantly sentenced him to death by crucifixion as a threat to the public peace that Pilate was responsible for protecting.

Jesus recast the meaning of righteousness, moving the emphasis from perfect human obedience to the law to faith in the divine compassion of God. This shift of emphasis, both conceptually and behaviorally, in the life and ministry of Jesus is what Moltmann calls the "staggering novelty" of Jesus.[2] Jesus' novelty continues to stagger conventional views of righteousness in the church and world today. His

---

2. Jürgen Moltmann, *The Crucified God* (San Francisco: Harper Collins, 1976), 105.

gospel, when truly grasped, was and remains countercultural. Externals of any kind—status, credentials, outward appearances in church and society—are illusory as benchmarks for measuring personal and institutional worth. The real measurements of worth rise precisely from the inner character and vivid actions of Jesus as the world's prototypical servant leader. The enduring benchmarks of worth are the capital qualities of servanthood that even worldly wisdom instinctively recognizes when we honor leaders of the human pilgrimage with Nobel Prizes, heroes of spirit and self-giving like Martin Luther King, Jr., Mother Teresa, and Desmond Tutu. Such leaders as these incarnate the attributes of Jesus: compassion, courage, and the closeness to God that forges high character from risk and suffering.

So, in a strange way, convention is both offended and lifted by the countercultural challenge of Jesus as servant leader. By examining prevailing cultural standards it may be possible to come to terms with the riddle of servanthood that continues both to offend and to exalt.

$$\infty$$

Jesus' emphasis on God's unmerited mercy was a radical undercutting of what theologian Marcus Borg calls the "purity code"—the code of social status and behavior that structured and controlled both the religious and social systems of first-century Judaism. The purity code derives from a particular meaning assigned to the Leviticus passage that calls Israel to the vocation of holiness:

> Speak to all the congregation of the people of Israel and say to them: You shall be holy, for I the Lord your God am holy. (Leviticus 19:2)

By Jesus' time, "holiness" had come to mean "separation." For the sake of their distinct identity as the chosen people of God, the Jewish people believed they had to separate themselves from everything unclean. Holiness thus meant purity: "You shall be pure, for I the Lord your God am pure." In postexilic Judaism the demand for holiness had evolved into an elaborate system for assuring and maintaining ritual purity for priests and lay people alike. This system was centered on the Temple, which had been rebuilt in 538 BCE, and was controlled by the Jerusalem priesthood.

This is the society into which Jesus was born and lived into manhood, a society built around a purity system, one that had centuries to develop before Jesus commenced his public ministry. Marcus Borg describes its public effect. Put very simply, a purity system is a social structure

> organized around contrasts or polarities of pure and impure, clean and unclean. The polarities of pure and impure establish a spectrum or "purity map" ranging from pure on one end through varying degrees of purity to impure (or "off the purity map") at the other. These polarities apply to persons, places, things, times and social groups.[3]

The outcome, Borg argues, benefited only the elite. The nonconforming majority was too poor to pay the Temple taxes on top of the heavy exactions against personal income by the occupying provincial government of Rome. The purity codes affected the whole economy, since certain occupations were categorized as impure (shepherds, prostitutes, tax collectors) while others were accorded special status by right of birth (especially priests and Levites, both hereditary classes).

---

3. Marcus J. Borg, *Meeting Jesus Again for the First Time* (San Francisco: HarperCollins, 1994), 50.

Other elites included the Pharisees and their lawyers (scribes), a mostly lay order whose very name means "the separated ones" and who strove for strict adherence to the law, ritual observance, and tithe-and-tax payments as the means of securing and sustaining purity status.

Jesus' rebuke of this professional hierarchy is highlighted in his condemnation of the hypocrisy of the scribes and Pharisees and in the vivid stories he told. Three of the parables are especially important in getting at the heart of the difference between his "code of compassion" and the purity code of the ruling and leading elite. All three parables are in Luke's account but nowhere else, suggesting that Luke's version of the gospel may represent the sharpest understanding of the revolutionary character of Jesus' challenge to the entrenched religious establishment of all times, his and ours.

The briefest of the stories begins, "Two men went up to the temple to pray..." (Luke 18:9-14). What ensues is the dismissal of the Pharisee with all his protestations of perfection, and the warm commendation of the despised tax collector, who offers his repentance as an ordinary sinner: "I tell you, this man went down to his home justified rather than the other; for all who exalt themselves will be humbled, but all who humble themselves will be exalted" (18:14). This is not a pious admonition to cultivate humility, as it is most often taken to mean, but a revolutionary rebuke. Jesus publicly scorns the legalism that separates people from one another. He rejects the moralism that is used to oppress those who are despised, to exalt a spirituality of self-importance, and to perpetuate the lines of social and religious distance between the clean and the unclean, the rich and the poor. All the compassion, courage, and risk of suffering (the real measurements of personal and institutional worth) are implicit in Jesus' bold invention of this story.

The second parable is offered in answer to a lawyer's question, "Who is my neighbor?" It begins, "A man was going down from Jerusalem to Jericho..." (Luke 10:25-37). Jesus then tells a brilliant tale about a victim of violence on the roadside and the reaction of three kinds of travelers who come upon the helpless (and apparently dying) man. Two of the travelers are members of the Temple elite, a priest and a Levite. The third traveler, like the tax collector in the previous story, is one of the despised, a Samaritan, a heretic from across the border. The two priests give the victim an anxious look and a wide berth, while the Samaritan performs a series of lavish acts of neighborly compassion.

Although this story ends with an admonition to be neighborly, its primary thrust is much deeper. As in the first parable, Jesus is hurling a vivid and masterful rebuke against a system that draws discriminatory lines between the righteous and the sinners. The priest and the Levite are not to be understood as cowardly, only self-protective in obedience to the prohibitions of their code. They are victims of their own spirituality. The scrupulosity of the purity code forbade their helping the robbed and bleeding traveler by its demand to avoid contact with the dying. Such contact contaminated a decent Jew's personal purity.

There is a further truth of servanthood in the story. The rebuke by Jesus of the purity code is made all the more radical by comparing the spiritual bondage of the conventionally religious with the exhilarating freedom of the "heretic." To get the full import of Jesus' meaning it needs to be asked: Who in the story is having the best time? Among the three actors in the parable, which of them would you choose to be: the priest, the Levite, or the Samaritan? Who is enjoying life the more: the scrupulous twosome or the servant leader?

The third story, longest of all, begins, "There was a man who had two sons..."(Luke 15:11-32). Everyone with a scrap of biblical acquaintance knows this ingenious story from the mind and soul of Jesus. The parable of the prodigal son, his older brother, and their compassionate father has been loved for centuries as a linchpin of Christian truth. It has been said that if we knew nothing else of Jesus but this single story we would know the meaning of the gospel of grace.

Like the two preceding tales, it too is *not* primarily a call to virtue. Instead, it serves the same bold purpose of Jesus—that of challenging the assumptions of a moralistic approach to God and goodness, the offending and threatening boldness of a compassion that led to his crucifixion. Actually the story is much more a vivid portrait of the Servant God than a commentary on human behavior, even though it does contrast the honesty of the wayward brother with the rigidity of the older sibling who has "never disobeyed" his father. The legalistic faithfulness of the older brother bears bitter spiritual fruit. It leads him not only to question his father and despise his younger brother, it also keeps him from the festive banquet. The same cheerlessness that we saw in the parable of the Good Samaritan is highlighted here too, suggesting the deep and dancing joy of Jesus. Betting his life on the embracing compassion of his Father, Jesus was free to see the law as fulfilled, not by strict and anxious compliance, but by the honesty of repentance and the offer of compassion to all others.

Such compassion, being the heart of Jesus' understanding of his Father, led him straight to joy. We know this not only from his valiant invitation to good cheer (John 16:33), but even more convincingly from the accusations of those whom he offended and threatened by his personal freedom and exuberance. He was vilified as "a wine-bibber and friend of sinners," openly violating convention by eating meals with tax collectors (Zaccheus) and prostitutes (Mary of Magdala). He feasted when the rule-book of the purity code called for fasting. He encouraged the violation of sabbath strictness by acts of healing on the very day that the behavioral code forbade it, defying a sacred requirement and assuring him of hatred by the cheerless. It is written that the common people heard him "gladly"—which could be translated from the Greek as "in gladness," meaning that they resonated in their spirits to his infectious joy. Edward Schillebeeckx, the Dutch theologian, wrote of "the existential impossibility of being sad in the company of Jesus."[4]

There is a piece of sculpture of two figures in close embrace in the bishop's garden of the Washington National Cathedral. One figure is leaning tenderly above the other, the other kneeling, half-hidden in the marble arms of a consummate caring. The slightest knowledge of the stirring parable of the prodigal son is all one needs for recognition. I stumbled onto this sculpture early one Sunday morning in 1960, before the eruption of social turbulence that has marked the American landscape ever since—but not before I, as a parish priest, began to awaken to an uncomfortable sense that the easy popularity of post-World War II "churchianity" was wanting. It lacked depth and breadth of discipleship, starting with me.

The sight of the statue that morning chastened and deepened my understanding and experience of God. On the instant of seeing it in a sequestered corner of the garden, with evergreen boxwoods behind it, I began weeping. It may not be great art—I have no credentials for measuring its worth as sculpture—but I knew in my soul that it spoke great truth. It conveyed the power of the mystical, the experience of being grasped by a transcendent reality. The initiative comes from beyond oneself and beyond one's anticipation; it simply arrives by surprise, and the impression becomes indel-

---

4. Edward Schillebeeckx, *Jesus* (Holland: Bloemendaal, 1974), 165.

ible, so that one can feel the very sensation of the moment, even years later. The statue seemed to capture the gospel truth of what I want to call "prevenient forgiveness." I mean by this phrase the encompassing compassion of God's embrace from long before it is sought—the tender mercy of God for all the world, from the very beginning of the world.

This is something that moralism has great difficulty allowing into one's heart. You hear the difficulty expressed in the impulse to side with the offended older brother of the parable. After all, he labored hard for years as a good and obedient son to do his father's bidding. Does he not have justice on his side in protesting the mercy of his father for the wastrel? He does indeed, if the measure of one's acceptability before God and the religious population is adherence to a strict code. And this helps explain why Jesus suffered rejection and crucifixion. He offended the righteous and threatened the security of a religious establishment that prospered by insisting that ritual requirements be scrupulously met—requirements like the payment of tithes and taxes and the offering of birds, sheep, and goats for sacrifice, the sale of which was controlled by the Temple hierarchy and its money changers.

Rembrandt painted a portrait of the parable, and this *is* great art. The original hangs in the Hermitage museum of St. Petersburg, where it was acquired in 1766 by Catherine the Great. Two features of Rembrandt's retelling of the prodigal son are important to the servant character of true power and the person of God as revealed in Jesus. The first is the suffering in the father's face; it marks his facial color, the angle of his body, and his half-closed eyes. The late Henri J. M. Nouwen sat for hours before the painting as part of a pilgrimage to Russia before his death: "Every detail of the father's figure—his facial expression, his posture, the colors of his dress and, most of all, the still gesture of his hands—speaks of the divine love for humanity that existed from the beginning and ever will be."[5]

Nouwen's insight into the father's hands is the key to a second feature of the painting. He points out that the hands portray a blend of the feminine and masculine in the character of God. The right hand is distinctly feminine with slender fingers, the left hand squarish with heavier fingers. We have no first-person singular pronoun to convey the mix of feminine and masculine in God—or in ourselves—only the words "he" and "she." But it is easy to foresee the development, in our everchanging language, of some word to convey the ontological blend of maleness and femaleness that C. G. Jung termed *anima* (the feminine) in men and *animus* (the masculine) in women. Rembrandt appears to have sensed this paradoxical mix of velvet and steel in the character of God long ago, the servant qualities of infinite tenderness and unyielding might that combine to make compassion the supreme power.

A third feature, which could not be expressed in either the sculpture or the portrait, both being fixed emblems of the story, is Jesus' description of the love that does not wait for a knock on the door. "While he was still far off, his father saw him and was filled with compassion; he ran and put his arms around him and kissed him" (Luke 15:20). Compassion is not a late blooming characteristic of God, but a love that existed from the beginning. Jesus as servant leader and revealer of God's truth is not Plan B, as if God were unprepared for the waywardness of humanity in sin and violence. Jesus is Plan A. Key passages of scripture make this plain. Paul writes of Jesus: "He himself is before all things, and in him all things hold together" (Colossians 1:17). The Crucified God is simply the eruption into history of the cosmic redemptive love that

---

5. *The Return of the Prodigal Son* (New York: Doubleday, 1992), 88.

is built into the structure of the universe from its start. The book of Revelation speaks of Jesus as "the Lamb slain from the foundation of the world" (Revelation 13:8, KJV).

If God were not vulnerable, if God could be protected from suffering and enthroned in bullet-proof majesty, such a god would be inferior to humanity. Humanity has the right to be skeptical of any god incapable of pain. Such a god is less powerful and less noble than humanity, because humanity takes on suffering and endures greatly for the very sake of loves that are imperfect. What this comes down to is that Jesus, in servant vulnerability to the pain of loving, is a God who can weep with us and for us. Human intuition knows that this is not weakness, but conquering strength. This truth is captured in the final verse of a new hymn from the pen of a contemporary theologian, W. H. Vanstone:

> Here is God: no monarch he,
>   throned in easy state to reign;
> here is God, whose arms of love
>   aching, spent, the world sustain.[6]

---

6. *The Hymnal 1982*, Hymn 585.

Chapter 5

Truth and the Servant Church

Let us dream of a church in which the Spirit is not a party symbol, but wind and fire in everyone, gracing the church with a kaleidoscope of gifts and constant renewal for all.
—Wesley Frensdorf

There is an old sea-story, probably mythical, about a whaling captain named Eleazar Hull. In the early 1800s Captain Hull was esteemed the ablest skipper in the whaling fleet that sailed from New Bedford, Massachusetts. He pushed out the farthest on every trip, endured the most punishing weather, returned with the biggest catch, and suffered the least loss of life among his crew. His record was all the more remarkable in that he had never been exposed to formal navigation training. Asked how he found his way in the trackless seas, he would reply, "When the skies are clear at dusk I go up on deck and rock slowly with the pitch and roll of my ship; then I listen for awhile to the wind in the rigging; finally I take a long look at the brightest stars. Then I go below to the chart room, fix my position, and plot my course."

Year after year Captain Hull functioned as the most skillful skipper of the fleet. The executives and directors of the whaling company continued to be happy with his performance until the fleet's insurance underwriters from Boston insisted that all ship captains be required to go to Harvard College for advanced training in navigation. The executives had to be agreeable, since otherwise the premiums would be heavily increased. But they worried about Captain Hull. He was a man of towering pride. Surely he would resist.

To their surprise Eleazar Hull responded with enthusiasm. He would love to go to Harvard, he replied, especially at company expense. Six weeks later, following intensive "continuing education" in the use of resource books, charts, technical instruments, and navigational nomenclature, he returned to his ship and put out to sea. Again he remained out the longest, sailed the farthest, returned with the biggest catch, and lost the fewest men. At the dock to meet him were the company officers and members of the board of directors.

"How did it go with your new learning, Captain?"

"It was wonderful," Hull exclaimed with a grin. "When the skies were clear I'd go up on deck with my sextant and clock, bring the required number of stars down to the horizon, mark the precise time and all that. Then I'd go below to the chart room and, using the data, mark my position from a three point fix—and then plot my course.

"After that I'd go back on deck, get the feel of the ship's pitch and roll, listen to the wind in the rigging, and take a long look at the stars. Then I'd go below to the chart room and correct my calculations." In Hebrew the name Eleazar means "helped of God."

This tale does not square precisely with the biblical experience of the Spirit that birthed the servant church, but it does fit with what we conjecture about the human brain and its capacity for knowing. We appear to have "left-brain" computation skills and "right-brain" intuitive gifts. It also fits the almost universal human experience of heavier reliance on "right-brain" guidance in the decision-making that shapes our lives. As the nineteenth-century poet Francis Thompson wrote,

> O world invisible we view thee,
> O world intangible we touch thee,
> O world unknowable we know thee,
> Inapprehensible we clutch thee.[1]

Left-brain and right-brain competencies in human knowing are part of a typology of truth that has slowly evolved in my mind over the years. I understand the term "typology" to mean a system that names the parts of a whole concept for purposes of clarifying the differences that distinguish the parts. I have used this typology in talks on servant leadership for business people. The system represents another way of explaining and integrating the religious and secular dimensions of life in an emerging understanding of power. Truth, when it is seen in its variety of expressions and levels of depth, is a way of integrating science and religion into a perception of the wholeness of truth, where science and religion are separate disciplines but basically inseparable in the wholeness of God-given reality.

The typology has six parts, each part defined with reference to its opposite and arranged in a descending order of depth. The first part is *empirical truth*. The opposite of a true fact is a false fact. Two plus two equals four, not five. While number systems are at a relatively superficial level in any hierarchy of truth, they are not insignificant. Empirical science proceeds on the basis of numbers as a dependable

---

1. Francis Thompson, "The Kingdom of God," *The Oxford Book of Christian Verse* (London: Oxford University Press, 1940), 516.

description of the universe. Numbers are the computational foundation of the world's most powerful knowledge base—the ground for the sciences that have altered the world and human life in applying and exploiting the insights of Cartesian/Newtonian mechanics.

After the empirical comes *relational truth*. The opposite of a true statement is a lie. This moves human knowing to a deeper level, for it either provides or erodes the foundation of relationships. Without truth relationships cannot long endure. The tragedy of Richard Nixon is evidence, along with the prevailing cynicism about government and most forms of authority today. Every lie I have ever told has, to some extent, injured the quality of my relationship to myself, to others, and to God. And every act of repentance, which means taking responsibility for the God-given freedom to choose, has been the necessary and miraculous first step in the healing of injured relationships. Repentance is the first invitation of Jesus to a claim on the kingdom of God. The kingdom is variously called in scripture the justice of God, the righteousness of God, and the peace of God.

Next in the typology comes *evolutional truth*. The opposite of a fixed truth is a truth that moves. As with relational truth, evolutional truth is not easy. Somewhere in the human make-up there is a deep resistance to whatever will not stay put. This is especially true of both science and religion as disciplines. The scientists of his day resisted the radical ideas of Galileo, and the church put Copernicus' works on the index of prohibited writings. A number of scientists today continue to resist the evidence and implications of quantum theory. Likewise, Christian fundamentalism cannot abide the conclusions of geological studies that reveal the enormous antiquity of creation. But there are fixed points in both science and religion. In science they are the principles of repeatability and the methodology of replication. In Christianity, while there has been wholesale movement beyond St. Paul's tacit sanction of slavery, there is permanence in his insistence on love as the fulfillment of every requirement of the law.

With *mythical truth,* the opposite of a factual truth of history is a story-interpretation of history that aims at history's meaning. On April 28, 1789 Fletcher Christian led the mutiny on HMS *Bounty* commanded by William Bligh: *this is historical fact.* The story of Adam and Eve was created by the genius of spiritual imagination to explain the tyranny of self-seeking commanders who blame others for the unhappiness of their command: *this is myth.* In the biblical story Adam and Eve are driven from Paradise, not because they disobeyed (they were still in the garden when confronted by God), but because they indulged their fear by shifting the blame to God, to one another, and to the serpent. In other words, they projected blame on all others available for blame, since the myth names only four actors (Genesis 3:1-24).

Paradoxical truth moves the typology to a deeper level. It says that the opposite of a great truth is another great truth. Briefly illustrated in the case of persons, paradox means that each of us is both an individual and a community. Individuality and community appear to cancel each other. Logically a person cannot be a singular entity and a plural entity at the same time. But the paradoxical reality is that every person is both at all times. It takes a human community to make a whole individual—all through life, from birth to death. Even at conception this is true, since it takes two to make one. And every single human being is a multitude of genetic and historical factors. The isolated simplex of a person is in reality a mind-boggling complex of forces in time and space. Thus it takes two mutually exclusive and apparently self-canceling truths to state the totality of what is true.

In 451 CE the bishops of the Christian church assembled in Chalcedon, a maritime town near the present Istanbul in Turkey. Their chief purpose was to find a way to state the church's conviction about the identity of Jesus as Lord and Savior. They concluded that the use of paradox was the only way to define the wholeness of the character of Jesus. They acted against the variety of partial definitions that vied as statements of orthodox Christian belief. So the bishops decreed Jesus to be simultaneously both fully human and fully divine. Similarly, servant leadership itself is a paradox. It blends contradictory human roles in dynamic balance as a way of stating the totality of what is true about a person who uses power to empower.

Mystical truth is the unsummoned presence of the beyond. I believe it is the deepest level of truth available to human experience. It means that the opposite of a grasped truth is a truth that does the grasping. The initiative in seeking and finding such truth is generally not one's own, but comes unbidden by human resolve or expectation. Every level of truth above this can be experienced, comprehended, and articulated, whereas mystical truth is confined almost entirely to the category of experience. The mystical, while common in human experience, cannot be fully comprehended or satisfactorily articulated. It is the sensation of being taken hold of in one's depth by an exalting power that lifts one's spirit above the ordinary.

William James, in his *Varieties of Religious Experience,* defines the mystical as "ineffable," meaning "beyond words." It is also beyond comprehension, at least in terms of the outlook that has prevailed in the West since the ascendancy of Cartesian and Newtonian science and metaphysics in the seventeenth century. The world-view put forward in our day by quantum physics, with its new perceptions of the natural order, insists on mystery and ineffability as inherent in scientific truth.

∞

Now I want to connect the experience of being grasped by the "ungraspable" with the rise of the servant church from the mystery of resurrection and the work of the Spirit that followed it. My starting point here is the unsettling reality of declining membership figures in many institutional expressions of Christianity. Almost every serious observer of the church today agrees that as an institution it has become marginal in contemporary society. The pieces of evidence for this evaluation are legion. For example, a "summit" meeting of American leaders was called together in Little Rock, Arkansas, by President-elect Bill Clinton in December, 1991. The purpose of the summit was to pool the wisdom and experience of the nation's eminent thinkers and practitioners for guidance in making policy decisions in the new administration. Almost two hundred men and women representing "the best and the brightest" in business, industry, law, medicine, higher education, public administration, entertainment, and sports spent several days assembling counsel for the President-elect and his Vice President-elect, Al Gore. Out of all these elite representatives not one was a theologian, ethicist, or parish minister. The absence of church leadership is all the more telling because both Bill Clinton and Al Gore are active and confessing Christians of the Baptist tradition.

This is "bad news" for our society, but only superficially. The deeper and better news is that the church was most vigorous when it was most on the margins. The vibrant early church was not only on the outer edge of acceptance until the embrace of Christianity by the Emperor Constantine, it was regularly scorned and periodically persecuted. From its bleak margins of social and political isolation, the church wrote the entire New Testament within a period of about seventy years, spread to the farthest horizons of the Roman Empire and the known world, and put in place the defining doctrines and ethical imperatives that have instructed and guided the enterprise of Christ ever since.

The early church on the margins sketches the paradigm of organized servanthood. The servant church in the first centuries after Jesus' death and resurrection reveal at least two attributes of servant power, attributes that must now shape the recovery of servanthood by a church newly marginalized: the servant church is *energized and shaped by the Spirit,* and the servant church is *emboldened to breach old boundaries.* The first attribute is an empowering innerness; the second is an explosive outwardness. One is the intensive energy of galvanizing commitment. The other is the extensive power of lavish inclusiveness that embraces the whole of humanity in a geography without boundaries.

∞

The first and foremost attribute of the servant church is its *daring openness to the Spirit* in fulfillment of what Jesus promised. The connecting passages between the Jesus of history and the Christ of faith are in the first chapter of the Acts of the Apostles. There the post-crucifixion Jesus is experienced as vividly alive and pointing to the future with promises of Spirit-bestowed invincibility:

> You will receive power when the Holy Spirit has come upon you; and you will be my witnesses in Jerusalem, in all Judea and Samaria, and to the ends of the earth. (Acts 1:8)

So vivid and real was the presence of the Spirit in the first generation of the servant church that the Acts of the Apostles was called "the Gospel of the Holy Spirit" by St. John Chrysostom, the eloquent preacher and fourth-century reformer who was the Bishop of Constantinople. The number of explicit references to the Holy Spirit in Acts is astounding. The Spirit is the precipitating actor at Pentecost and in so many reported episodes in Acts that the conclusion is inescapable: the servant church at its birth and thereafter is Spirit-seized, Spirit-shaped, and Spirit-guided—almost never without tribulation, often in internal conflict, always in the energizing oversight and care of the Spirit. The presence of the Spirit was the source of the servant church's compelling power to bring about personal and social transformation.

So active is the Spirit in the primitive servant church that Pentecost is not simply a one-time event. The Pentecostal phenomenon is repeated in at least two passages. Luke reports:

> When they had prayed, the place in which they were gathered together was shaken; and they were all filled with the Holy Spirit and spoke the word of God with boldness. (Acts 4:31)

Likewise, in the testimony of Peter before the Roman centurion Cornelius and his household there are distinct Pentecostal elements:

> While Peter was still speaking, the Holy Spirit fell upon all who heard the word. The circumcised believers who had come with Peter were astounded that the gift of the Holy Spirit had been poured out even on the Gentiles, for they heard them speaking in tongues and extolling God. (Acts 10:44)

Clearly, the Spirit's work is the building and restoring of community.

The Christian theological tradition from the start has assigned the work of "oneness" to the Spirit. In terms of human sensation, when the mystical sense of being deeply at one with life and with God is experienced, especially in the joy of a broken relationship reconciled, this is the work of the Spirit. Forgiveness is somewhere at the heart of this mystery: the compassion of God that holds all life in an embrace of love and that awaits only the readiness of repentance to be experienced as an inner lilt. Since childhood I have treasured the verse of scripture that says simply, "He restoreth my soul" (Psalm 23:3), which is the healing work of the shepherding Spirit.

"Oneness" itself comes before all else. Oneness is the basic order of creation from the beginning. Science now understands this from a quantum perspective and speaks of the cosmos as a living organism of interconnectedness. From the start of God's creation we live in an interwoven world of pulsing "inter-being," all things linked in interdependence with everything else. Moreover, an understanding of cosmic reality as *fields of interconnection* suggests a fresh grasp on the biblical meaning of sin. Sin is the arrogance that prompts and perpetuates alienation. Teilhard de Chardin defined evil as "disunion"—living in willful separation from the whole of things. Evil is the condition of "dis-integration." Sin is thus human collaboration in the "dis-ease" of a "broken-apart" (fallen) world. By this insight, long perceived by theologians and now substantiated by a quantum grasp of the cosmos, sin is the willful disposition to *disconnect.*

The work of the Spirit, then, is to *reconnect.* The human soul is reconnected to one's larger self, immersed and fulfilled in the experience of community. This is what the human soul is made for, and in its moral freedom is continuously

called to claim by repentance. Repentance, in this understanding, is the noblest posture and loftiest act of human
freedom. It is the human soul owning up to responsibility for
the free choices that injure and sunder the community of life.
Repentance is the human soul's "suffering itself" into the joy
of community recovered.

There is a cherished Christmas story about this transaction of the soul—this suffering oneself into the joy of reconciliation. In *A Christmas Carol* Charles Dickens has graced
the world with his portrait of humanity in bitter alienation
and at last redeemed into the transporting glee of community recovered. If we were not all, to some degree, Ebenezer
Scrooges, the story would not be the classic it is. "Bah hum-
bug" is Dickens' dark sacrament of speech that signals alienation. Dickens is a shrewd psychologist: Scrooge's
bitterness rises from a soul deeply wounded by parental
scorn and neglect in a lonely childhood. This is the hidden
root of his rage at Bob Cratchitt for requesting a day off at
Christmas and his contempt for the plight of the poor—
along with his tart dismissal of his nephew's invitation to
celebrate Christmas with the family. Then comes the long
night of enduring a painful review of his alienated life, beginning with "the Spirit of Christmas past," who leads Scrooge
through a rehearsal of his boyhood. Dickens uses "spirits" to
confront Scrooge with the pageant of his life in dis-connec-
tion. It is a night of ardent repentance in which Scrooge
accepts responsibility for his disconnecting choices and the
habits of alienation that flow from them. He begs for the
chance to reconstruct his life—and from his repentance receives the gift of being reborn.

When he discovers on waking that it is still Christmas
morning, Scrooge can scarcely contain his joy. He throws
open his bedroom window and asks a passing lad if the
Christmas turkey is still in the window of the butcher shop,

and, being told that the turkey is there, congratulates the boy for his perspicacity and dispatches him on an errand of generosity to the Cratchitt household. The rest is familiar—and perennially soul-restoring, even though we have heard the details a hundred times and know the ending, even as we know the details of the gospel tales of Christmas. Not only are the Cratchitts blessed from the riches of a soul restored, but the nephew as well, and all whom Scrooge encounters on the city's streets in the course of that luminous day. All of London was brightened by the generosity that flowed from one man's repentance and God's compassion.

∞

The second great work of the Spirit is the building and restoring of community. That is why the second attribute of the servant church is the *boundary-shattering work of inclusion.* The record of this is again found in the Acts of the Apostles, the chronicle of the servant church at its adventuresome best. Chapters 8, 9, and 10 of Acts tell three stories of inclusion that aroused conflict.

In Acts 8 the apostle Philip baptizes an Ethiopian, a man excluded from the Jewish community because he was an alien and a eunuch. In his sacramental action Philip has violated an explicit prohibition of the Deuteronomic Code, which expressly forbids the inclusion of a mutilated male in the sacred assembly: "No one whose testicles are crushed or whose penis is cut off shall be admitted to the assembly of the Lord" (Deuteronomy 23:1). But Philip, daring a disobedience to the niceties of the law, laid aside the old prohibitions, entered the water with the eunuch, and embraced him in baptism. This is the extensive power of the Spirit's lavish inclusiveness.

In the ninth chapter of Acts it is the disciple Ananias, on the street called Straight in Damascus, who breaches the boundaries of caution to welcome a highly suspect candidate for baptism. Saul of Tarsus, savage persecutor of the earliest Christians, while on an errand of retribution commissioned by the Jewish council, experienced a life-altering experience of unbidden mystical power on his way to the city and was instructed by the Spirit to find Ananias and ask for help. Ananias is instructed by the Spirit to offer welcome to the persecutor. Naturally he is abashed and resistant:

> But the Lord said to him, "Go, for he is an instrument whom I have chosen to bring my name before Gentiles and kings and before the people of Israel."...So Ananias went and entered the house. He laid his hands on Saul and said, "Brother Saul, the Lord Jesus, who has appeared to you on your way here, has sent me so that you may regain your sight and be filled with the Holy Spirit." (Acts 9:15-17)

In that very private moment, who could have foreseen what would result from the daring inclusion of an energetic genius like Paul? His writings testify to the fact that his restlessness, harnessed thereafter to the Spirit, compelled him on an evangelistic journey that covered as much as twenty-five thousand traceable miles on the roads and sea-lanes of the Roman Empire.

In the tenth chapter of Acts it is Peter who dares to violate the boundaries by including one of the truly despised in first-century Palestine, a high officer of the occupying Roman military.

> In Caesarea there was a man named Cornelius, a centurion of the Italian Cohort, as it was called. (Acts 10:1)

Cornelius was a devout man, and when he heard of the preaching of Peter he sent for the apostle in order to know more of the new word of God spreading through the territory. At the same time, Peter had been instructed in a dream not to call profane anything that the Lord has made clean and to go with the men who would be looking for him. When the men sent by Cornelius arrived in Joppa, Peter agreed to go with them, taking with him some Jewish companions and believers in Jesus. They arrived the next day at the centurion's house in Caesarea, where many had assembled. Invited by Cornelius to speak, Peter began by emphasizing the inclusiveness of the gospel:

> You yourselves know that it is unlawful for a Jew to associate with or to visit a Gentile; but God has shown me that I should not call anyone profane or unclean....I truly understand that God shows no partiality, but in every nation anyone who fears him and does what is right is acceptable to him. (Acts 10:28, 34)

He then proceeded to tell the story of Jesus' ministry, crucifixion, and resurrection from the dead. While he was speaking, the assembly of Gentiles received the gift of Spirit and spoke in tongues. Peter baptized the entire gathering. In the mystical power of the moment, he was given the boundary-shattering courage and compassion of the Spirit.

Later in Acts is the record of internal conflict evoked by the boundary-breaching power of the Spirit. The fifteenth chapter of Acts tells of the wrenching controversy over the relationship of Jew and Gentile. The infant church decided to uphold the actions taken earlier, without official sanction, by the Spirit-moved leadership of Philip, Ananias, and Peter—and later by Paul. In that first "General Convention," called by the leadership in Jerusalem, a compromise was worked out that allowed for the inclusion of Gentiles in the church and the honoring of certain ritual and behavioral mandates long required of faithful Jews.

This call of the servant church to be daring in its inclusivity continues to stir controversy today. The Episcopal Church has endured the same kind of boundary-shattering controversies during the nearly fifty years I have spent in ordained leadership within it. At every General Convention I have attended since 1958, when we argued feverishly over the issue of installing the biblical tithe as a standard of stewardship, we have faced similar challenges of "inclusion." Since then we have had to struggle repeatedly against the exclusionist impulse that tends to intimidate us all. That impulse wanted first to deny women membership as deputies to the Convention; then it fueled the fierceness of debates over racial integration in the church. When we moved to embrace our black brothers and sisters into full church membership and leadership, the first of the modern-day schisms erupted when small minorities of Episcopalians formed break-away churches. Next came the fierce controversy over including contemporary expressions of worship in the liturgical offices of *The Book of Common Prayer,* a controversy that continues to ferment in small corners of the church and which prompted the formation of still more break-away churches. After that, we argued and decided in favor of including women in ordained leadership, an action that continues to threaten Episcopal unity.

Now we face what many believe will be the most passionately resisted call of all—the acceptance of gay and lesbian sisters and brothers into the church as pastors and leaders. This critical issue has penetrated all the Christian denominations, and is one of the challenges that mark our moment in history—the overarching challenge being to shift our understanding and use of power from domination to participation. Churches deal with this pressing sexual issue in a variety of ways: some face it immediately, in spite of its divisive thunder, while others resist even talking about it.

No matter what our personal stance on these and many other issues that threaten to divide us, we can help one another stay open to the Spirit and to seek to bring light and healing while moving ahead in love and justice. Nowhere in scripture is there a commandment to be right—only to love. Even—or especially—in our differences, we as servant leaders can be faithful to the finest in the tradition of the servant church, "that wonderful and sacred mystery" as our liturgy describes it.

The chapter that follows is a true story of the Spirit's reconciling work in using the ministries of a community of servant leaders among the church's laity.

Chapter 6

Servanthood in Conflict

*It's enough to give you whiplash, trying to comfort the
frightened traditionalists with one hand while reaching
out to the enlightened seekers with the other. It would be a
whole lot easier to ignore one group or the other, which
many churches have decided to do, but if you ask me, the
stretch is an occupational hazard. It is just what you do
when you are living between the end of one world and the
beginning of another.*

—Barbara Brown Taylor

I was ordained in 1949. It was a good year to begin work in
the church. World War II was over, I was out of the navy and
finished with seminary. Ike was soon to be president, and the
church burgeoned in the suburbs where a postwar housing
boom built new neighborhoods almost overnight. The only
things really difficult about being a priest and pastor in those
halcyon days were sermon preparation and wedding rehearsals.

Making ready a sermon was always "a pain in the mind."
It started slowly every Monday morning and ratcheted up in

spurts of anxiety like rising thunderheads that blew themselves out on Sunday morning. Twenty hours of toil were
condensed into a polished monologue of about twenty minutes, and a few kindly folks asked for a copy at the church
door. The sermons got easier to crank up through the years,
but I could never simply "toss one off." Every Monday morning I felt like I was drawing on a half-empty rain barrel with
one little minnow near the bottom. The wedding rehearsals,
however, did yield to the transforming magic of sound management when I added a "wedding hostess" to the parish
staff. Or perhaps I added to the duties, with a pay boost, of
the most extroverted and stylish of our three parish secretar-
ies. Whichever it was, the move turned wedding rehearsals
into pleasant interludes of watching a skillful woman handle
the temporary madness of the wedding party.

All in all it was fairly easy to be an ordained minister until
the 1960s. Then everything changed when Martin Luther
King, Jr., forced us to pay attention to the civil rights movement. There was no way to avoid a new and, for many people,
painful choice: we were either with him or against him. Some
of us were there cheering in Washington when King finished
his historic "I Have a Dream" address, but the church's official response was what could have been predicted from an
institution whose social presence and behavior is essentially
conservative. Change always arouses conflict in an institution with roots deep in tradition, and the civil rights movement was among the first of the convulsions of change in the
modern church that have been with us ever since.

Yet despite the pain there is both grace and gain in all this
confrontation. When I was a young priest in the 1950s our
church conflicts were hopelessly trivial. We argued passionately over the merits of costumes, candles, and other cus-
toms in high church and low church practice, and whether
we must do without breakfast before the early morning Holy

Communion service. In these latter years, since the erup-
tions of the sixties over civil rights, we have moved steadily
from preoccupation with church practices and ecclesiastical
trivia to concern for public and ecclesial justice—and in the
process we have developed a splendid moral muscle.

Still, as Barbara Taylor points out, the leadership of today's church is suffering from a chronic case of *whiplash*. For
more than thirty consecutive years we have had to struggle
to combine, if we could, the extremities of conservative and
liberal conviction in congregations and dioceses more or less
traumatized by unrelenting change. This has been hard, but
not unhealthy. Church conflict is discomforting, but not un-
suitable to the church's purpose. Nor is it unhistoric: conflict
has always accompanied the spread of the gospel, and taught
us something about its impact. Our own era of conflict has
again revealed two searching and undeviating truths about
Christianity.

First, the gospel is countercultural. Taken seriously, Christianity will always put the status quo under sharp moral
critique, personally and collectively, because at the heart of
it is a challenge to all self-seeking: to save your life you must
lose it, as the gospels report the central challenge of Jesus
(Luke 9:24). The earliest history of the church, the Acts of the
Apostles, is a story of ceaseless conflict. The church was born
in the agony of crucifixion and grew swiftly against the pains
of unrelenting opposition from both the Jewish establishment and the Roman state. An axiom emerges from the
fires of institutional stress: *Servant leadership never splits the
church; it only exposes the divisions that are already there,
opening them to the reconciling work of servanthood.*

The second truth that our era of trauma has forced into
the open has to do with the authority of leadership. In most
arenas of church life it is now no longer possible for leadership to commend itself on the basis of external credentials.

Just being an elected lay leader or a bishop or a priest will not cut the mustard with a leader's constituency or sisters and brothers among the ordained. Authority now must rise from deep within the character and quality of a person's soul, for without an evident depth of integrity the authority of election or ordination in and of itself simply does not carry weight for most church people. Sadly, many people appear to be dropping out of church life when they experience leadership that lacks inner conviction and power. George Gallup's research shows that the single largest segment in the religious population of America is made up of what he calls the "decoupled"— those who continue to cherish a belief in God but who no longer attend church. This may be a just retribution: spiritual and moral mediocrity in leadership eventually receives what it deserves by way of mediocre response and respect.

In the New Testament, the principal word for authority, *exousia*, is translated as "strength of character," not as "official position." We know this from two New Testament sources, one of them linguistic, the other personal. The Greek word *exousia* literally means "out of being"—rising up from the depths of one's authenticity as a person, the authority of one's force of soul. The other source for a true understanding of authority is in the person of Jesus, of whom it is written that "the crowds were astounded at his teaching, for he taught them as one having authority, and not as their scribes" (Matthew 7:28-29). He carried no institutional credentials. All that he had to commend himself was his luminous innerness, his oneness with God.

To carry this kind of authority, to which ordinary people responded with astonishment and joy—and sometimes with bewilderment—is also to risk the hostility of those with official power. The religious leadership of Jesus' day reacted to him with fear and rage. Real authority certifies one as an

Alter Christus, a Christic presence to others, a person of truthful, prayerful, self-giving servanthood to God—to the church and to the world. This, I believe, is the deepest meaning of the name servant leader: *Alter Christus.* It is also what Christians pray to become. One of the eucharistic rites of the Church of England says it best: "Fill us with your grace and heavenly blessing, nourish us with the body and blood of your Son, that we may grow in his likeness."

To "grow in his likeness" is to become more each day a person of steel and velvet. Hidden in the stress of *whiplash* is the gift of growing into Christlikeness in one's own unique way. Since the 1960s the Episcopal Church has been stressed by the struggle to hold together frequently hostile factions: on the one hand those of our people who are energized by change and on the other those whose passions are fed by the familiar. Clergy who have used this stress as raw material for inner growth are often the direct beneficiaries of the servant leadership of their laity. God has given us people in our congregations whose grace and grit have empowered their clergy.

∞

My experience of growth through conflict started several years before that August day of 1963 when I thrilled to the rolling eloquence of Dr. King during the March on Washington. Six years earlier, in 1957, it became apparent that the boom in church attendance following World War II would force the church I served, the Church of the Redeemer in Baltimore, to consider renewing its worship life with a new church building. We had been worshiping since 1858 in a modest fieldstone Gothic building with a slave gallery at the back and a tall stone steeple on its own foundations near the front door. The building was designed to seat about two hundred people in a pinch, and by extending one of the transepts we added roughly one hundred more seats in 1955. The congregation continued to grow. By 1957 we numbered fifteen hundred families and had to use the chapel-size worship space four times every Sunday morning: 7:30, 9:00, 10:30, and 12 noon.

It was time to look for an architect. In doing so we found an *Alter Christus* among us, though we did not know this until we ran into the high winds of architectural controversy. Had we known in advance that his vision would stretch us to the point of pain we would surely have chosen another. But his leadership as a servant changed both the outward and inward character of a fine congregation of Christians.

Knowing that we could temporize no longer because of our numerical growth, a committee of the vestry was formed. Their first task was to produce an illustrated brochure with ground-level and aerial photos of our nine-acre tract, along with a text that told the parish history and explained our current challenge. This document was sent to fifteen architects across the country, inviting those interested in a commission to visit with the rector and committee on site in Baltimore at their earliest convenience. Eleven of the fifteen responded and made the trip, including such well-known architects as Marcel Breuer and Walter Gropius. Eero Saarinen was unable to take on more work at the time and declined to come, but the Dean of Architecture at M.I.T. was our first visitor, Pietro Belluschi.

Mr. Belluschi, a native Italian who had emigrated to America in his early twenties, had won fame among architects for his sensitive creativity, especially in the design of churches. He made a distinct impression on us when we met him: he seemed at home with us immediately. Handsome, gracious, and deeply intelligent, he carried a quiet, almost self-effacing competence about him. He was unhurried as he inspected our little church and its related parish buildings, remarking appreciatively on the simplicity of the whole composition of structures and their nine-acre setting. I was charmed. So was everyone on the vestry committee.

In the following weeks the committee interviewed all the remaining ten architects in turn, but they came back to Pietro Belluschi. The choice was easy. More than any architect who had visited us he expressed admiration and respect for the existing village-like church. He insisted that whatever new facility was designed, by whomever, it must take its leading architectural idiom from the little church's simple Gothic lines, allowing its commanding steeple to remain unchallenged as the exterior climax of a new and larger composition of buildings. Subsequently he accepted our commission and, on the basis of our confidence in the choice, the vestry proceeded to raise a great sum of money. But subsequent to the successful fundraising, which exceeded its goal, a storm of trouble developed. It began to blow when Mr. Belluschi submitted his plans.

We assumed we had an architect of traditional Gothic tastes, since he had evidenced such warm respect for the little church, but we were radically wrong. His design called for deep transepts flanking an outthrust chancel with a free-standing altar, purple carpeting in all the aisles and covering the entire chancel area, horizontal windows running the complete perimeter atop interior stone walls, a forty-foot high altar screen of over one hundred different colors of fist-size chunks of stained glass stretching from the floor to a steeply angled hardwood ceiling supported by interior massive arches of wood laminate. This was an earthquake to a comfortable, conservative congregation with a rector whose easy conservatism had never before been seriously examined. Only the interior Gothic arches fulfilled Mr. Belluschi's promise that the basic architectural idiom of the existing church would be honored—plus the great steeple as the exterior climax of a cluster of old and new buildings.

The committee developed a strategy which they hoped would help diminish the gale force of the winds they knew would begin to blow. A grand model of the nine-acre tract was built using exquisite scale reproductions of the old and proposed new buildings, with all the trees in fetching fall colors. The model was mounted on a concealed pedestal in the parish house and rotated slowly as the focus of avid parish attention for three months. In this way we sought to defuse the mutiny that was brewing while awaiting a visit by Mr. Belluschi to address a series of parish meetings to explain and defend his design.

The strategy worked with many, especially with the young. But among the great bulk of the senior membership, the good people who had given and pledged by far the most money in the campaign, a polite fury boiled. It seemed to me a cultivated pretense of some segments of Baltimore society. I came to understand that icy affability as an oxymoron, a "genial hostility." It was coiled and ready for Mr. Belluschi's visit.

He came on a Tuesday evening in February, 1957, during the dark and gloomy leading edge of Lent. (By some who were present it was designated "Black Tuesday" thereafter.) In his address Mr. Belluschi spoke of the long tradition of Christian architecture, fitting his conception into the evolution of patterns of sacred space. He explained that a particular meaning of his design was to put a large number of people in closer proximity to one another and to the center of sacramental worship than would be possible in a conventional cruciform arrangement. He also said, with a warm smile, that we could have any color of carpeting we wanted—as long as it was purple!

When he finished and asked for our response, the first questioner was the chair of the altar guild, a brave and forthright woman. She stood to challenge the architect. She began, "Mr. Belluschi, I speak for many in this congregation when I say...." A preamble of this kind in response to an address tends to arouse an inner karate posture in the speaker. Even though it may grossly exaggerate the number of people represented in the challenge, it always sounds like an angry army coming over the hill. "I speak for many in this congregation when I say," she continued, "that your design simply doesn't look like a church."

It was a moment when a lesser person might have demolished the woman. As a scholar and historian of architecture he could have made her look like a fool by his grasp of the range of symbols and idioms that sensitive artists have developed over the centuries of Christian worship. He had the power to intimidate and humiliate, to dominate and coerce. He chose not to use that power—probably not as a conscious decision, but as an expression of his own inner being. He answered her out of his authority as a servant leader, not his standing as the Dean of Architecture of a prestigious institution. He said, "I know what you mean, and I need you."

As I recollect, he went on to say, "An architect who is sensitive to what is new and everchanging can become self-serving and even bombastic in the use of symbols—designing something that has no connection with the tradition out of which we come as Christians, the tradition that has nourished us in the love of God. The great temptation for a contemporary church architect is to propose something with little sense of the reminiscent and familiar. So I need you, lest I design arrogantly and with no respect for the ages of our faith. I thank you for your courage to challenge me, and I honor your own sensitivity to our Christian heritage.

"But it is also true," he continued, "that you need me, lest you forget that we worship a living God, and that what we decide to erect in this time and place must not implicitly declare before the world that we gather in a museum of religious artifacts. The God of our faith is one who insists that we be on pilgrimage, giving us places of abode for sustaining our journey, as in your lovely little church, but whose voice continually summons us, *Follow me*. Just as you would have no patience with your rector were he to speak in Elizabethan English and use illustrations only from thirteenth and four-teenth centuries, so too you ought not to countenance an architect who would neglect to be as creative in our own time as were the honored designers of our past. What you build on the corner of Charles and Melrose in Baltimore needs to be an *evangel*—a sturdy and beckoning witness to the living God in Jesus Christ. What we need to do here is to preach a high-hearted sermon in stained glass and stone."

The chair of the altar guild, true to her grace and bravery, stood again at her place to make a reply, without a trace of hostility. "Mr. Belluschi, I need to say emphatically that it still does not look like a church—but you are the most charming man I have ever met."

Resistance to change and the overcoming of resistance is not basically an institutional issue. It is personal. It only takes on institutional form because that is how individual persons relate to one another. Margaret Wheatley has a marvelous insight into this:

It seems to me that resistance always reflects the need of each of us to understand who we are at the moment, our identity. When we see a change being forced upon us, we recognize it as threatening our sense of self. Resistance reflects our need to protect our sense of dignity and identity as presently defined. Resistance does not represent a fundamental tendency toward inertia, which is an old belief about human nature....If identity is a key issue, then it seems to me inescapable that we involve people from the start in whatever the change is going to be. Then they have a chance to reorganize their own sense of identity to fit the changed reality. You can't change people, but people change all the time. That's who we are.[1]

What our architect did in his response to the altar guild chair was to engage an important spokesperson for the institution and, by honoring who she was, give her space for reconsidering and reordering that identity. This seems to me a key expression of the *power of participation*. He invited us to participate in his power by honoring the implicit power in the position of the resister. And he did it by taking the lead in acting out what I believe are at least two clear paradigms of servant power.

The first paradigm is the inevitable tension between a dream and the prevailing reality. This tension can be visualized as a rubber band stretched vertically between the exploratory vision of a creative leader and the less adventuresome attachments and habits of mind of the people being led. The task of servant leadership is to maintain that tension and simultaneously to embrace both the dream and the people, in order to move the attitudes and attachments of the people up in the direction of the dream. When this happens a new reality can come into being. It is the fruit of the costly struggle to be faithful to one another in the tension of exchange between

1. Margaret Wheatley, "The Unplanned Organization," in *The Noetic Sciences Review* (Spring 1996).

the leader's vision and the people's natural resistance. In this way reality itself is changed in living response to the dream, while the dream itself is refined by the participation of the people in responding.

The second paradigm of servant power is implicit in the response of the leader to a challenge by those being served. Mr. Belluschi's response provides a vivid clue as to how the tension created by a great dream acting on a resistant people can generate the energy to bring about a new reality. This paradigm also has three parts, embodied in the simple sequence of the servant leader's answer to the altar guild chair: *"I have a dream. I need you. You need me."* This three-part pattern suggests the personal attributes of the servant leader in action, qualities that mark the innerness of an *Alter Christus*. They are seven distinct capacities, and together they form what could be called "the seven C's" of servant leadership.

1. Call. This is the mystical grasp of the Spirit in the leader's soul. Call is the high sense in the heart of the leader that the leader is *also* being led. It is the strong prophetic component in all leadership—the vision, the distant goal, the long view over the horizon. It is the insistent sense that what is not yet *can yet be*, can be summoned into being with enough patience and help from others. For our architect, the call was his daring conception of a yet unrealized sacred space that blended tradition with something utterly new. For Jesus, as the *Christus* in whose image servant leaders are called to be shaped, the call is the kingdom of God. The kingdom of God was his dream of a new community, a new world, and the centerpiece of his summons to discipleship.

2. Communication. Communication is the sharing of the dream in a hundred different ways over time, in pictures and parables and propositions. It was in Mr. Belluschi's drawings and the quietly rotating model in the parish house. It was in his coming from his citadel at M.I.T. to be with us and risk our outspoken distaste of his dream. We know what communication was for Jesus. His stories and challenges—and the acting out of his servanthood *unto death*—will continue to illumine the way ahead, lift our hearts, and echo down the corridors of Christian witness as long as there is human speech.

3. *Compassion.* Compassion is "feeling from the other side." The Greek of the New Testament has a marvelous word for it: *splanknidzomai*—literally, "gut feeling." The *King James Version* of the Bible translates it as "the bowels of compassion." For our architect, compassion was in his refusal to use his considerable power to scorn or diminish someone who didn't agree with him. It was in his feeling for the sensibilities of a dream-resister. His compassion also included the rare capacity to discern in resistance an ingredient of crucial value to the process of creating something new. Jesus' compassion was his constancy in reaching out at great personal cost to the despised and marginalized—to women and children, the sick and the disfigured in body and soul. Compassion also figured in his accessibility to anyone from the ranks of the socially powerful who wanted contact with him, as in the case of Nicodemus and Simon the Pharisee. While his main regard was for those who were disregarded by society, Jesus' embrace included all of humanity.

4. *Command.* This is essentially the work of holding others to account as morally free human beings created by God with two moral capabilities: to be personally responsible for their choices and to grow up. Command is never blaming. Blaming is the automatic reaction of accusation and denial. Blaming is always possible, but it cancels collaboration and reduces trust by putting spiritual distance between the leader and the led. Blaming evokes the energy of alienation, reducing the freedom and courage of both the leader and the

led. Command rises from the energy of reconciliation, of warm belief in people, of seeing the best without denial of the worst. Command is the energy of uniting a person with a vision of what that person is capable of achieving—in taking responsibility for personal behavior and growing beyond the limits of suffocating fears and conventional perceptions. In a single word, command is the work of stretching people to new heights as Pietro Belluschi stretched us—although not all at once. His servant spirit of velvet and steel put in place the dynamic of trust and affection that made it possible for people with only conventional vision to move to a fresh and expanded embrace of beauty. This is the meaning of Jesus as one who commands: "God did not send the Son into the world to condemn the world, but in order that the world might be saved through him" (John 3:17).

5. *Compromise.* Compromise expresses the maturity of the servant leader. The ability to compromise rises from the leader's recognition that those who are led have within them facets of creativity which, if allowed incorporation into the leader's dream, will enlarge the dream's own truth. Compromise is often made to sound like surrender, like giving ground in weakness. This is because our values have been corrupted by a world-view that reduces creation to disconnected parts and pieces—including people in their fundamental relationships. In such a world-view the isolated individual has a prior value over community. We have been seduced into believing that competition is the great driving force of human achievement. It is not, and never was.

Collaboration is the real energy of human striving and accomplishment, not competition. Modern research in the field of anthropology confirms that the human species is genetically coded to cooperate; we have survived and advanced as a species because we are built to rely on one another. Anthropologist Richard Leakey points out that collaboration is what makes possible the savagely competitive enterprise of war. Troops advancing shoulder to shoulder, *in disciplined collaboration*, is more fundamental to organized warfare than war itself. Even more primitively, humanity as a species is distinguished from less specialized orders of life by the advance of collaborative hunting and gathering over random competitive individual grazing.[2]

Once we grasp the fundamental importance of collaboration, then compromise means gain, not loss, because inclusion of the strength of others is enhancement for any important dream. It is also the way of obtaining a win/win outcome. Seeking to include others in decision-making as a way of making wiser decisions radically changes the way we listen to others. In a competitive win/lose relationship, we hear in the arguments of others only what we can hope to discredit and demolish. In a collaborative win/win relationship we seek to hear in the arguments of others those ingredients we can affirm for the enrichment of the outcome.

Mr. Belluschi returned to M.I.T. to rework his design after his meeting with us. Jesus listened to the plea of a Syro-Phoenician woman whose bravery led him to redesign his vision. Her appeal that he heal her daughter, though not a Jew, enlarged the boundaries of his mission to make it inclusive of all the nations—a compromise to which *he appears to have been stretched* in a brief instant of encounter on the road (Mark 7:26).

6. Cruciformity. Leadership involves suffering. When exercised with love and courage leadership bears the cross. Every leader knows this cost. The human spirit recoils at the idea, but can it be imagined that Jesus endured his cross to spare us ours?

---

2. Richard Leakey, *Origins* (New York: E. P. Dutton, 1977), 284ff.

The inevitability of tension between the dream and prevailing reality is the real pain of the dreamer. The tension rises out of all the coiled and determined impulses of human resistance to change—all the rejection of the leader, all the fear and contempt of what is different, all the calumny to which prophets have been subjected in all of history. Without love from many quarters the leader's work would be too painful to bear, which is a clue to the measure of extremity in Jesus' suffering, losing finally all close support in his abandonment by the chosen few around him. But such suffering love cannot be defeated in God's cosmic design. Death in the divine economy makes room for life. God is the author of life on both sides of death. Trust in this truth is what shines in the servant leader.

7. *Cheer.* Or more accurately, "good cheer." In the Sloan School of Management at M.I.T. the good cheer of the leader is likened to the skill and buoyancy of spirit in a good sailor. Teachers there point out that a fine sailor can use any wind that blows as the power for making headway, coordinating the destination and the prevailing wind currents while adjusting the sails to tack this way and that. The only wind a good sailor cannot use is *no wind.* This implies that leadership at its best will always raise the winds of controversy and tension by daring to dream, using that very tension as the driving power for a journey to new horizons. Our architect was such a sailor, along with his team of local architects. They used the winds of the congregation's response to tack on a good course, teaching us and learning from us so that the final plans were all the better for being shaped by the storms that blew.

The word for "good cheer" in the language of Jesus is translated in many versions of the New Testament simply as "courage," while other translations use "heart": "In the world you face persecution. But take courage; I have conquered the world!" (John 16:33). Here conquering means overcoming the *principalities and powers* of the world, which are the powers that seek domination and control, enthrall the proud and the privileged, and lead to oppression, economic injustice, and the violence of war. These are the dark energies that deprive both the powerful and the powerless the joy of evoking the powers of love and servanthood that are built into every human soul—and that await their calling forth by a quality of being in the world after the manner of Jesus as an *Alter Christus*, a servant leader. This is the genuine good cheer of the saints. In the fourteenth century Julian of Norwich offered her most quoted salute to the conquest of the principalities and powers: "All shall be well, and all shall be well, and all manner of thing shall be well."

∞

Though it still "didn't look like a church" to many, in the end the church was built, purple carpet and all. It happened this way.

An impasse developed in the vestry. Most of the sixteen men (no women in 1957) continued to resist the Belluschi design. In meeting after meeting no one budged. Finally they decided to find out what the congregation wanted, so ballots were prepared and mailed to every household that simply asked a single question with two alternative answers, "Which do you prefer, that we proceed with the Belluschi design, or that the vestry engage another architect?"

Perhaps a month later the vestry met in a closed and highly charged session to receive the results. The tally on the balloting had been kept a matter of strict confidence until then. When it was reported that over one thousand ballots had been returned and that the tally was seventy-seven percent in favor of the Belluschi design and twenty-three per-

cent opposed, the atmosphere in the room tensed percepti-
bly. Discussion revealed that the percentages in the vestry
were almost precisely the reverse of the congregation's: four
vestrymen favored the present plan, twelve were opposed. A
twenty-five to seventy-five percent split the other way.

The eighteenth-century Vestry Act in the State of Maryland, under which the vestry of an Episcopal Church is legally
designated "Corporation Sole," absolves a vestry of all legal
accountability to the membership of a parish. In other
words, the vestry could do as it pleased. As I recall that
evening, our discussion became heated and then softened as
the hour grew late. Finally one member, a great citizen of the
city and chairman of the trustees of the Johns Hopkins University, stood and offered his personal testimony.

"All of you know," he said, "that my wife and I are offended
by the design proposed by the architect. And you may sur-
mise that we gave generously toward a new church, believing
earnestly in the need for it. Most of you also know that we
have children, along with their children, in this congregation. What you cannot know without my telling you is that all
of them, children and grandchildren, are keenly in favor of
what we, their parents and grandparents, oppose. They all
wish us to proceed with the architect's proposal. As for percentages, I myself did not know this until tonight, but their
wishes and ours are almost exactly the split of percentages
in the parish. They are seventy-five percent and we are
twenty-five percent in the Garland family. Aurelia and I have
pondered this and prayed about it earnestly. In the process
it dawned on us that of the Garlands we two will be around
the least amount of time to worship in whatever building we
erect. They are the ones who will worship in this parish the
longest of us all. We believe we must honor their wishes. I
move that, as a vestry with an undoubted moral obligation

to the people of this parish, we proceed with design of the architect."

Immediately there was a quiet "Second" from the circle, and then silence. I called for discussion of the motion. Silence. Someone called the question. I asked if that was the wish of the vestry. Silence. I called the question. "All in favor say aye." Muted voices responded all around the circle. I was astonished at the number. "All opposed." Silence. "All who wish to be recorded as abstaining." Silence. There were a few tears of quiet emotion around that solemn circle, and nothing more to do except to pray, which we did, and then adjourned into the night.

I still cannot write of that event without emotion. The evening's outcome, and the whole odyssey of moving a congregation into new territory, remains my earliest and most enduring experience of beholding the exquisite grace of servant leadership in the church's laity. It continues to move my soul to recall a living demonstration of the truth that "real power is the exchange of power."

Chapter 7

Servanthood and Sexual Ethics

Time makes ancient good uncouth....
—James Russell Lowell

L owell is only partly right. Time does erode the worth of some "ancient goods," but hardly all. Time confirms more deep good than it can ever make obsolete. The older I grow the more I am gripped by the enduring truth and power of the gospel of Jesus Christ. Its good news promises that when we can break the oldest of human addictions, that of confessing other people's sins ("blaming"), and take responsibility for our own behavior ("repentance"), then we enter the door to a cosmic compassion that has been open since the beginning of the world and life begins anew.

Repentance is simply personal truth-telling. Truth-tellers experience freedom from fear and pretense, a gift of the gospel that is impervious to change. Nowhere in our time is the gift more needed than in the area of human sexuality. In this chapter we will explore servant leadership within institutional conflict by focusing on the difficult question of blessing gay and lesbian relationships. The issue is so disturbing for millions of good church people that their impulse is to turn away—or to turn to scripture and argue that the question was settled long ago. People who take the Bible literally maintain that while scripture allows concern and discussion, any deviation from scriptural prohibitions is not permitted. Since that is what I used to believe myself, I am writing to share a personal pilgrimage that has taken me from there to an entirely different place in my understanding.

The first principle for the guidance of servant leaders in institutional conflict, set forth in the previous chapter, is the *honoring of a dream.* My dream is of a church reborn to compassion and inclusion. It is this commanding dream that prompts the sharing of my odyssey.

The second principle in dealing with church conflict as a servant leader is the *honoring of those who hold an opposing view*—not simply out of kindness, but far more out of the practical recognition that the church could not be faithful without respect for the gift of tradition. We make our way forward by facing backward, as in a rowboat. Therefore the discussion of a new Christian view of sexuality needs the presence and input of those fellow pilgrims who hold tradition dear—lest, in our pursuit of a dream, the old landmarks be lost to view and we lose our way as the Body of Christ. This understanding uses the paradigm of the architect Pietro Belluschi: "I have a dream. I need you. You need me." I need the traditionalists to guard me against overstepping the boundaries of faith and goodness. Traditionalists need me, and many others of like mind, lest they fail to step up to the widest parameters of love and justice.

It may be thought that a challenge to traditional morality is an act that divides the church. I disagree. A forthright challenge like this exposes the divisions already among us. Exposing alienation—getting it out where we can face it—makes possible the reconciliation to which we are called as members of Christ. Reconciliation presupposes alienation by the very meaning of the word. Thus a frank facing of alienation is the essential precondition to its overcoming in reconciliation.

Reconciliation does not mean agreement on an issue. It means letting go of anger. It means the refusal to treat one another as apostates and enemies of Christ. It means finding the patience and courtesy to hear one another and so to learn from one another. Reconciliation means obedience to the controlling commands of our religion: that we practice loving God by loving one another. Christians are never at liberty to nurse alienation, never. There is no commandment to be right. The binding commandments, on which "hang all the Law and the Prophets" according to our Lord, are the commandments to love. Since there is no commandment to be correct, I believe this means that Christians are not only free but obliged *to risk being wrong*—for the very sake of the law and the prophets that mandate love as the highest ethic in our tradition.

I want to go back now to Lowell's claim that "time makes ancient good uncouth." Most contemporary Christians can agree on certain clear cases where tradition or moral convention has been superseded. What was once an unchallenged moral value can, over time, be exposed as false, even immoral. Human slavery is one of these cases; the author of Colossians 3:22 ("Slaves, obey your earthly masters in everything...") clearly suggests tacit approval of slavery, or at least no strong objection to a practice that today is not only morally inadmissible, but a punishable crime in most countries of the world. The position of women is another such case. The view that women were created inferior to men, and deserve no place in church or public responsibility, is now contemptible. In other words, we do not walk untrodden ground. Pilgrims before us have repudiated or refined earlier values in favor of those more "true and fitting" in the light of moral and spiritual growth.

In 1977, as Bishop of Atlanta, I wrote a lengthy pastoral letter to the diocese. It was heavily laced with biblical, historical, theological, ethical, therapeutic, and scientific references and ran to nineteen pages, closely typed. In it I advocated a traditional position on the issue of homosexuality, which was then beginning to surface as an issue in the churches. More specifically, I was attempting to address the founding of a gay and lesbian network called Integrity in the Diocese of Atlanta. Integrity was founded in 1974 by an extraordinarily gifted young professor of English, an Episcopalian who was teaching at the time in one of the colleges in middle Georgia.

The key statement in my pastoral was this: "I propose that there be mounted a ministry of healing to the homosexual...to seek replacement of the homosexual condition, be it either ambivalent or fixed, with a decisive heterosexual orientation." The letter was greeted with mighty applause, both in the diocese and widely throughout the Episcopal Church and beyond. The conservative ecumenical journal *Christianity Today* reprinted it in full and dispatched it to the far corners of their subscriber coverage. It was even translated into Swedish and became an official statement of the Lutheran Church of Sweden. The approval was delightful, but I wondered when the counterattack would come. It never came. Instead, the only response from the gay community in Atlanta was wounded silence, punctuated by overt expressions of disappointment in their bishop, but no counterattack or angry rebuttal. Just the reverse. In response they invited me into a personal and sustained conversation. "Come be with us," they said. With some misgivings, I went.

When I wrote the original pastoral statement in 1977 I knew only one gay person well, the professor of English. He frightened me with his penetrating challenge that he was as complete a human being as I—in fact more so, because in order to be openly honest about his identity he had to face public contempt and the censure of his church. Self-acceptance for him required far more courage and suffering than my self-acceptance was costing me. In the area of sexuality, his claim to a more complete and courageous humanity was patently true.

In the years since my earliest close encounter with a Christian who was gay, my fear has slowly dissolved. The heavy walls of unexplored prejudice have come down—those walls behind which I hid and tried to deny by lobbing balls of quietly conditional love over the top to the "prisoners of perversity" inside. Since that invitation of 1977, I have come to know large numbers of gay men and lesbian women, many of them clergy. I have heard them speak from their anguish of alienation and their heart's deepest truth. We have worshiped together repeatedly. In almost every case they have told me, in one way or another, that from their earliest sexual arousal they were moved by someone of the same sex. Most characterized the attraction as strong and commanding; many fewer said that there seemed to be a bisexual element in their attractions. Sexual desire thus appears to run along a continuum, a spectrum of emotion and attraction, with the heavy majority of humanity positioned decisively at the heterosexual end and a significant minority positioned just as decisively at the homosexual end, with many fewer somewhere in the middle.

The pained and patient testimony of good and faithful people, gathered over years of encounter with a long-suffering segment of the Christian community, is the foundation of my changed point of view. I no longer believe, as I once did, that homosexuality in most people is a voluntary pattern of behavior, or something that is amenable to change. Instead, I believe that such attraction is ontological, by which I mean it is a morally neutral *bestowed* identity for the decisively gay and lesbian person.

This view is supported by a growing body of scientific research and opinion. It insists that a small but not yet clear percentage of the human species, from time immemorial, has come into life with a homosexual stamp of identity. Many earnest conservatives claim that the scientific community removed homosexuality from the list of psychic dysfunctions for political reasons, and that a powerful minority maneuvered its approval. I do not know whether this claim is substantiated by solid research, but I am aware that it is widely disputed by a large body of respected therapists and medical practitioners. Most important to me from a personal standpoint is the overwhelming testimony of gay and lesbian persons, gathered from many years of close pastoral contact with them, which points me heavily in favor of support for the action of the professional therapeutic community in removing homosexuality from its list of amenable neuroses.

A friend who is a priest of the Episcopal Church and has spent his adult life in holy orders has given me permission to quote from his moving and confidential 1996 Christmas letter. He writes of his recent sabbatical:

> With plenty of time to reflect and read, I began to realize what God was trying to help me comprehend about myself. I began to accept the truth that I've been spending an enormous amount of spiritual energy to deny and hide from my sexual orientation. Once I let go, I knew an overwhelming sense of freedom and peace, and of grati-

tude. Walking the Labyrinth...revealed all kinds of ways in which my life has been limited and hindered because I actually believed that I could choose not to be gay. Truly accepting that it's not a choice, and that God has a role for me which includes this dimension of who I am, has been so wonderfully liberating. There's nothing physical involved—it's not that I've become attracted to some particular person. It's a deep letting go of my life-long attempts to control who I am, instead of just accepting what God has provided.

Many of us have begun to see what the Quakers understood about homosexuality years ago—that it is an ontological characteristic of birth, a "given," like race or gender. Quaker devotion to the Spirit has pushed them "ahead of the curve" in compassion and social justice for a long time in their history: they freed their slaves a hundred years before the Civil War. In deciding on the full and legitimate humanity of homosexual persons, Quakers understand, as serious Christian gay and lesbian people themselves understand, that all sexual identity carries with it a high ethic of fidelity and life-long intent.

Why do we not bless partnerships marked by the same qualities of friendship and fidelity that we celebrate as the most cherished attributes of a sturdy Christian marriage? Why are debates on this question marked by such bitter invective in the church? One of the barriers to understanding and agreement among Christians on matters of sexuality is our nearly two centuries of shyness in talking about sex at all, especially in theological and moral dialogue. The first letter of Paul to the Corinthians, written in the first century, set a precedent for centuries of Christian sexual austerity:

> To the unmarried and the widows I say that it is well for
> them to remain unmarried as I am. But if they are not
> practicing self-control, they should marry. For it is better
> to marry than to be aflame with passion. (1 Corinthians
> 7:8-9)

At best, our tradition has been ambivalent about human
sexuality, relishing in private what it will not discuss in public—except, of course, as fuel for scurrilous jokes. What we
cannot talk about easily, we joke about vulgarly.

So the Bible is one source of our difficulty with sex. Present history also makes it difficult to think soberly and com-
passionately about a departure from sexual tradition.
Anxiety-free Christian dialogue on sex is profoundly inhib-
ited by the so-called sexual revolution of our time. The contemporary outbreak of sexual permissiveness may well be in
direct proportion to the repressive attitudes that have long
prevailed in societies shaped by Christian moral seriousness.
The rising tide of divorce, family disintegration, domestic
violence, and the increase of infectious diseases, including
AIDS, all combine to make it difficult to assess with an open
mind any new challenge to sexual convention in church and
society.

However, the negative side of the sexual revolution is not
inherent in the priceless gift of sex, but in the human perversity that drives us to abuse all the gifts of life. In terms of
sexual abuse, permissiveness has had far more dire consequences in the straight population than in the gay, simply
because the former are so more numerous. In considering
the question of the legitimacy of gay and lesbian relationships and commitments, the dialogue needs to be lifted
beyond both repression and permissiveness. Deliberately
choosing the inner posture of servanthood can cancel, or at
least reduce, the impulse to use the power of moral convic-

tion to dominate, manipulate, or pour scorn on anyone. It should help us to claim the vocation of servanthood in this debate by recognizing that both sides agree on one point: *sexual profligacy, promiscuity, perversity, and adultery are out of bounds for any Christian.*

A further barrier to sober dialogue and possible agreement is the long historic attachment of marriage and sexual intimacy to the procreation of children. The marriage rite of *The Book of Common Prayer* reads:

> The union of husband and wife in heart, body, and mind is intended by God for their mutual joy; for the help and comfort given one another in prosperity and adversity; and, when it is God's will, for the procreation of children and their nurture in the knowledge and love of the Lord. (BCP 423)

Represented in that preamble to the marriage rite is a profound historic change in the Christian view of marriage. The change is implied in a new sequence of the purposes of marriage. For centuries the purpose of marriage was held to be threefold: first, the procreation of children, second, the mutual support of the contracting parties, and third, the stabilizing of the social order. But that order of priorities could not remain unchanged in a changing world. People live far longer, human population has exploded, and birth control has become an imperative.

Interestingly enough, these realities were anticipated by a sensitive Anglican ethicist as early as the sixteenth century—not for reasons of overpopulation, but for the deeper reasons of human spiritual purpose and fulfillment. In 1551 theologian Peter Bucer criticized the first English prayer book for its conventional assertion that the first purpose of marriage is the procreation of children. Not so! said Bucer. The first purpose of marriage is the mutual good of the marrying parties—and after that in importance are children and the social order.

Almost four centuries later Episcopalians made Bucer's insistence a matter of canon law. The 1949 General Convention enacted a canon requiring people seeking to be married in the Episcopal Church to sign a Declaration of Intent that reads, in part "We believe [marriage] is for the purpose of mutual fellowship, encouragement, and understanding; secondly, for the procreation, if it may be, of children...; and for the safeguarding and benefit of society." This reordering of the purposes of marriage profoundly reevaluates the place of sex in marriage. Henceforth sex is best seen as serving the first purpose of marriage, "the help and comfort given one another."

This means that an enduring same-sex partnership cannot, in and of itself, violate the moral purpose of marriage. On the same grounds older people can marry and, in strict moral obedience, decide against having children. Younger couples may do the same. Despite heavy disagreement among Christians about the appropriateness of same-sex unions, at least three benefits can flow from a new sexual anthropology. First, it reduces the power of accusatory judgment of one another, that vivid symptom of angry projection and fear. Second, it strengthens the grip of Christian sexual imperatives of monogamy and fidelity as applying equally to every kind of union. Third, it contributes to the stability of society by making it socially acceptable to enter into same-sex partnerships that are bound by commitments to monogamous faithfulness and life-long intent.

Another, and perhaps the biggest, barrier to good and reasonable dialogue on this issue is our promise in the Christian tradition to be faithful to Holy Scripture, which includes the prohibitions found both in Leviticus and St. Paul on homosexual behavior. Leviticus 20:13 states that two men who lie together "as with a woman" must be put to death. This statute parallels other savage penalties for behavior that undermines the mandate to honor family ties and procreate for the sake of tribal survival, so it is imperative to see these passages in social and historical context. Similarly, the first chapter of St. Paul's letter to the Romans comes down hard on homosexual behavior, as it does on a whole catalog of waywardness in people: "full of envy, murder, strife, deceit, craftiness, they are gossips, slanderers, God-haters, insolent, haughty, boastful, inventors of evil, rebellious toward parents, foolish, faithless, heartless, ruthless" (Romans 1:29b-31). I do not think that Paul could have been referring here to the same kind of behavior that the church is being urged to bless—the sexual union of committed and faithful couples. Love and commitment cannot possibly be a part of Paul's catalog of condemnation; there is no way to practice envy, murder, strife, deceit, craftiness, gossip, God-hating, and slander in goodness and love. Instead, what Paul appears to be doing in his lavish list of sins is establishing a prelude to his promise of equally lavish mercy: "For all alike have sinned, and are deprived of the divine glory; and all are justified by God's free grace alone, through his act of liberation in the person of Christ Jesus (Romans 3:23-24, REB).

Once the social and historical context of these kinds of prohibitions is understood, then a more nuanced use of scripture is called for when we look to it for ethical guidance. The Bible was not written in a vacuum: the God of scripture is a God of history, anchoring Christian theology and ethics in the realities of the world, not as in the case of the mythical deities of ancient Greece. The influences of their gods were seen as coming from outside time and beyond history. Not so the God of the Bible. God trods the earth, as in the story of the man and the woman in Eden: "They heard the sound of the Lord God walking in the garden at the time of the evening breeze" (Genesis 3:8). God is present, not only as overseer, but as protector and lover: "He will feed his flock like a shepherd; he will gather the lambs in his arms" (Isaiah 40:11).

By including homosexuality in his catalog of perversity, however, with no distinction between identity and behavior, Paul does establish a position that is extremely hard for a modern Christian to maintain. In my view, compassion demands some middle ground. This is what I tried to find in my 1977 pastoral letter, before coming to my current conviction about the ontological character of homosexuality. My earlier position was this: while homosexual behavior is prohibited in the church, homosexual orientation is a regrettable defect and not part of God's intention. Therefore, I argued, it is subject to treatment. If treatment doesn't help, then total abstinence is required. This was in keeping with Paul's admonition: "To the unmarried and the widows I say that it is well for them to remain unmarried as I am" (1 Corinthians 7:8). So, I wrote in the original pastoral, *it is all right to be but never to do.*

But if homosexual orientation is involuntary, a bestowed identity, then what do we mean when we say that it is all right to *be* but never to *do?* This amounts to saying that it is all right to have blue eyes but not to use them for seeing, because sight is reserved for the majority of people who have brown eyes. If it be denied that homosexuality is a bestowed identity, like blue eyes or brown, or black skin or white, then condescension on "being" homosexual and prohibition on "doing" homosexuality remains the only acceptable Christian position, both now and into the foreseeable future. But to more and more of us, many of whom are parents of homosexuals and fast friends of homosexuals and bishops and priests to homosexuals, such a hardened position seems the triumph of fear and stereotyping, the imprisoning use of scripture and the perpetuation of injustice. As the numbers of people who have accepted the ontological reality of gay and lesbian identity grows, the question becomes whether we can live with this divided conviction indefinitely. When do we make a decision? And how? What kind of decision will suffice to hold the church together? This brings me to my final emphasis in this chapter: How can divided communities move ahead in decision-making about difficult issues?

∞

After a commitment to pray for the church and for one another across all lines of division, the most important thing we can do is to clarify what the church continues to stand for. The thought of the church changing a long-held sexual ethic has the potential of raising a whole host of related questions about long-held beliefs. If we can change our view of sexuality, what else can change? What does the church stand for anymore? To what do we hold fast in the high winds of this turning point in time?

The first answer has to be the "summary of the law" as laid down by Jesus and repeated in the liturgical manuals and worship practices of nearly every Christian tradition. "Thou shalt love...." The second answer would be to hold up the historic creeds that are included in most corporate Christian worship rites: "We believe in one God,...maker of heaven and earth, of all that is, seen and unseen. We believe in one Lord, Jesus Christ...." The third answer must lie in some form of baptismal covenant that commits the baptized to work for world peace, social justice, and the dignity and worth of all human persons regardless of their status, race, behavior, and allegiances. In the Episcopal Church the newest baptismal formula asks a piercing question of each candidate: "Will you strive for justice and peace among all people, and respect the dignity of every human being?" (BCP 305).

These three answers are the foundation on which we stand. Beyond these essentials, there are three historic points of clarity that may have the power to hold us together and move us to higher ground during this debate. The *first* is the fact of St. Paul's own liberality. Far from being rigid in his writings and his admonitions, Paul warned against any tendency to make an idol of his letters. In his first letter to the Corinthians he wrote a heart-lifting invitation to freedom in response to his teaching:

> So then, my dear friends, have nothing to do with idolatry.
> I appeal to you as sensible people; form your own judgment on what I say. (1 Corinthians 10:14-15, REB)

Fifteen centuries later an English theologian, Richard Hooker, also urged the use of human reason in discerning God's will, when he wrote that the Holy Spirit will "direct men in finding out by the light of reason what lawes are expedient to be made for the guiding of his church, over and besides them that are in scripture."[1] A slavish literalism with regard to scripture can betray a need to impose human control on God. *The fearful impulse to seek control of God and others, from which all of us need deliverance in order to truly love, may be nowhere more evident than in the selective and literal use of scripture to deny others the gospel gift of freedom.*

The second point of clarity that may help in community decision-making is to see that conflict has troubled the church from its first generation. Not all "irreconcilables" have led us into schism, and those that did split the church can be said to have strengthened and clarified the enduring

---

1. Richard Hooker, *Of the Laws of Ecclesiastical Polity, Book Three,* Folger edition, 235.

core of truth in the ancient catholic tradition. Many contro-versies of the early church over the nature of God and the meaning of salvation pained the church but did not impede its course as evangelist and reconciler. Even the violent ref-ormations of the sixteenth century brought new strength—both to the Reformers in their fidelity to scripture and to the Catholic contenders in their allegiance to a reformed papal authority.

The *third* point of clarity that may help get the churches beyond these "irreconcilables" in the debate over human sexuality is a growing readiness to look more deeply into our own hearts—where fears and unexamined darkness may block the power of the church in its vocation to be, in Robert Greenleaf's words, "the enlarger and liberator of her people." Parker Palmer defines a leader this way: "A leader is a person who has an unusual degree of power to project on other people his or her shadow, or his or her light."[2]

All of us remember those classrooms of our youth where shadows predominated and others where light and energy prevailed. The inner life of the teacher may have made all the difference—whether love or dread dominated her or his spirit. The heaviness of a class in college chemistry still hangs around as a vividly remembered gloom for me: I can almost smell the acrid chemicals in Dr. C's lab. By contrast, I had a professor of comparative anatomy whose love of young peo-ple and formaldehyde was so infectious that I still remember the names of muscles and bones in the bodies of dogs and cats and humans. I even find the odor of formaldehyde fetch-ing. What created the light in Overton T. Ballard's lab and not in the other? I remember the first teacher as a man of lofty and rigid "rightness" about his subject matter as well as

---

2. Parker J. Palmer, *Leading from Within* (Washington, D.C.: The Servant Leadership School Press, 1995), 2.

about his politics and his religion, which crept into his classroom by innuendo. I have no idea what Dr. Ballard thought about politics or religion—as an anatomist and geologist he must have appreciated Darwin and the theory of evolution—but of his love of teaching and his encouragement of others in finding out things for themselves, I am very sure. It will always warm my heart to think of that inspirer in a white lab coat who enlarged and liberated me by the power of his splendid innerness.

Why is it so hard to go inside for what deeply moves us and communicates darkness or light? I think it is because our leadership traditions teach that "externals" are what count: doctoral credentials and published books in academia, profit margins in business, large congregations and complex dogma in churches. These externals help us leaders keep our fears out of sight—we think. But others can see them—and feel them.

There is a long and unfortunate tradition in the church that closeness to God means distance from sex. In Christianity sex is more often tolerated as a necessary evil than celebrated as a gift from God. But the rising tide of acceptance in the churches of homosexuality as a *bestowed* identity is a sign that the church is slowly moving from embarrassed toleration to the celebration of sex as a gift from God. It is my belief that the churches could advance the celebratory embrace of sexuality by blessing same-sex partnerships that are marked by the same quality of friendship and life-long fidelity that we celebrate as the most cherished attribute of Christian marriage. And indeed some churches have already broken the bonds of fear and acted with the courage of the servant church, as they extend to same-sex partners the same pastoral support and encouragement given to heterosexual couples.

Institutions that are willing to die to their own rigidity, and suffer through the pain of reform, regain strength and blossom anew. "Very truly, I tell you, unless a grain of wheat falls into the earth and dies, it remains just a single grain; but if it dies, it bears much fruit" (John 12:24). Death is a precondition to life, both here and hereafter. The phenomenon of dying to the smaller dimensions of understanding in order to enter a new level of love and knowledge is discernible at so many points in the odyssey of the Christian community, beginning with the first "general convention" in the fifteenth chapter of Acts. We Gentile Christians would not be around to argue and endure the "disturbance of our peace" were it not for the decision in the first century to include us as we are—not requiring that we submit to circumcision and become Jews in order to follow Jesus.

The energy of God's Spirit in servanthood reveals itself in all the provocative and fragmenting church issues of the closing years of this millennium. What remains to be encouraged in facing the controversies over human sexuality is a compassion that refuses to demonize or exclude anyone, even those who decline to be included and instead threaten to break away in anger and accusation. The highest form of servanthood is the nonviolence of what Jesus taught in Matthew's condensed rehearsal of his truth:

> You have heard that it was said, "You shall love your neighbor and hate your enemy." But I say to you, Love your enemies and pray for those who persecute you, so that you may be children of your Father in heaven. (Matthew 5:43-45)

Such a quality of serving others is never finally achieved. The grace of inclusion is a process of advancing spiritual maturity. It comes of honest sharing and prayer in community with others whose companionship girds Christians for life-long learning in the vocation of servanthood.

Part III

∝∾

Servant Leadership
in the World

Chapter 8

Servanthood in Work and Business

What gives power its charge, positive or negative, is the quality of relationships. Those who relate through coercion, or from disregard for the other person, create negative energy. Those who are open to others and who see others in their fullness create positive energy. Love in organizations, then, is the most potent source of power we have available.
—Margaret J. Wheatley

Work is holy because God is a worker. The world as the arena of life is God's handiwork, and creation is an ongoing process. Perhaps the most astonishing thing about God's work is that, for all the awesome regularity of earth's rhythms in the flowering of life from the seas and the soils, there is so much that God invites humanity to take up as co-creators. Meister Eckhart, German mystic of the fifteenth century, put this truth with startling boldness: "God can do as little without us, as we without God."[1]

---

1. Quoted by Harry Emerson Fosdick in *The Meaning of Prayer* (New York: Association Press, 1962), 60.

God heaps the hills with stone but never built a cathedral; God fills the earth with ore but never made a needle or a cookstove. George Eliot imagines the joy of Stradivarius in his work:

> When any master holds
> 'Twixt chin and hand a violin of mine,
> He will be glad that Stradivari lived,
> Made violins, and made them of the best
>   ...For while God gives them skill
> I give them instruments to play upon,
> God choosing me to help Him.
>   ...If my hand slacked
> I should rob God—since He is fullest good—
> Leaving a blank instead of violins.
>   ...He could not make
> Antonio Stradivari's violins
> Without Antonio.[2]

Work is the principal arena of our leadership. Work is therefore the arena of our servanthood—in homemaking, parenting, and decision-making at every level of responsibility in any enterprise, profit and nonprofit alike, as well as in the astonishing and blessed *busyness* of retirement.

Americans are being forced by two contemporary circumstances to do some rethinking about work. One, there are fewer midlevel jobs today because of big-business downsizing. Two, we are beginning to understand that money is not the principal satisfaction most people derive from their work. These two realities are strongly linked. They relate to the spirit of work—whether our work is a participation in God's work of creation, for which the human soul appears to be made, or whether our work is an alienation from participation and creativity, and thus an experience in soul suffo-

---

2. *Ibid.,* 61.

cation. Having a job is not the same as having satisfaction in work.

The nature of work is the real issue, not the provision of jobs. As the old kind of jobs get scarcer we will be compelled to muster a new kind of creativity that can turn a bane into a blessing. Job scarcity is forcing an increasing number of people to invent their own work, and as a result they are discovering that inventing their work is the best way to enjoy working. Tertullian, a Christian theologian of the second century, knew this secret when he said, "Where our joy is there should our work be." Another philosopher, this one of our own time, told her children, "Do what you want and the money will follow." We need most to find out what we *want* to do and then ask God for the courage to find out *how* to do it. And then to practice patience while we do the finding.

Everybody needs money, and everybody needs to work. Yet between money and work there is a surprising disconnection: the two only appear to be linked. On the surface it looks like money and work are joined like the two handles of a pair of pliers; one without the other makes the tool useless. But the metaphor of plier handles applies only to the connection between *jobs* and money, not to *work* and money. When Robert Reich, a professor at Brandeis University and former Secretary of Labor, asked a wide variety of people in a survey whether they would work if they inherited enough money to live comfortably, roughly eight out of ten answered "yes." This explains what has seemed a puzzlement: that almost all lottery winners, after a few months of champagne and a suite at the Ritz, end up punching the clock again—if not at their old jobs, then at some other.

When *Fortune* magazine asked scores of managers, from CEOs to warehouse supervisors, why they worked, all of them responded that the number one reason was to pay the mortgage. Beyond that, the three most common reasons cited were, in this order: to make the world a better place, to help themselves and others grow spiritually, and to perfect their technical skills. Putting aside the obvious connection between working and providing a home, the other three reasons, particularly in their surprising order, pinpoint what is crucial in human work: to serve the common good and one's own need to grow in spirit and skill.

We need to be clear about the huge difference between jobs and work. *A job is something somebody else defines. Work is something you define for yourself.* In most businesses we speak of having a "job description." This makes a job something handed down by management. Work comes from an altogether different place—not from higher up, but from deep within. Work is what the soul of humanity is made for. God works, not without ceasing, but with time-out for a sabbath exultation over what God's creativity has wrought. Science now perceives the universe as an ongoing evolution; humanity is made in the image of this working (and sabbath-resting) God. That is why work that fits a person's soul feels more like fun than toil. That is also why retirement, for most of us, becomes so full of happy work that we wonder what we did when we were working! Here is the essence of the difference between the level of fulfillment in a job defined by someone else and work you invent yourself.

Courage to find what really fulfills one's soul rises from a quality of innerness that may take a long time to develop, but is exactly the view of reality that Jesus tried hard to encourage. He insisted on the view that abundance is the name of the game, not scarcity. A playfully respectful paraphrase of Matthew 6:25-34 would read: "Don't you know that God is on your side and will never let you down? He has the whole world in his hands, and the world turns on an axis of compassion and plenty. There is a far better way to be rich than to have lots of money. The better way is to have simple wants and heaps of gratitude. Look around you at the rich and poor, and you will see that simplicity and thanksgiving make the poor rich, and that the absence of these interior habits of faith make the rich miserable. O you of little faith! (The equivalent of saying, "you turkeys!") God knows your needs. So take heart and kick the habit of anxiety. Put God at the center of your life, trust God's goodness, practice a persistent gratitude, and all that you need will be yours—including a sense of being alive in the commonwealth of God with a good work to cheer your soul and provide for your children."

In his book *Working,* Studs Terkel wrote, "I think most of us are looking for a calling, not a job. Most of us have jobs that are too small for our spirit. Jobs are not big enough for people." Servant leadership is a calling that is big enough for people—a work large enough to enlarge and liberate the soul and to fulfill Jesus' paradox that undergirds all happiness: that to lose your life in servanthood is to find your life.

How do we find this calling? What does it look like to be a servant leader in the world of work? Robert K. Greenleaf has done more than any leader in business circles to help us see what servanthood means in that arena. In his first and seminal essay, *The Servant as Leader,* written in 1972, he fashioned a now famous "test" by which to measure the meaning and effectiveness of the servant leader:

> Do those served grow as persons; do they, while being served, become healthier, wiser, freer, more autonomous, more likely themselves to be servants? And what is the effect on the least privileged in society; will they benefit, or, at least, not be further deprived?

Greenleaf himself was employed by AT&T for thirty-five years. For most of those years he worked in the field of management development and education, retiring as Director of Management Research. Perhaps the most remarkable

thing about his famous "Test for Servant Leaders" is the fact
that the context out of which he fashioned it was his experience in American business—not the family, not the school,
not the church. He intended *business itself* to be a prime
nurturer of servants. In his vision the proper vocation of
business includes, but goes far beyond, financial health. Its
purpose involves the fostering of spiritual well-being. Therefore the highest calling of any business is to see itself as a
servant to society in developing people committed to serving. Furthermore, Greenleaf insisted that leadership in business cannot be counted successful without a positive care for
the least privileged in society, so that they will "benefit or, at
least, not be further deprived." What we have in this remarkable statement is a holistic approach that includes a genuine
concern for individuals in their need for personal autonomy,
as well as care for the social order in its need for compassion
and justice.

This emphasis on relationships in business squares with
the slow recovery in our time of the "perennial wisdom" that
understands the universe as a network of interconnectedness. Reality is relational, not mechanical. At its deepest level
the leadership of others is a matter of spirit—of loving one's
people, not mastering them, because the mystery of living
relationships is the central characteristic of the cosmos.

In the early 1980s *Psychology Today* reported on research
done by The Center for Creative Leadership in Greensboro,
North Carolina.[3] Two behavioral scientists at the Center,
keen to discover the personal qualities and skills that make

---

3. Morgan W. McCall and Michael M. Lombardo, "What Makes a Top
   Executive?" in *Psychology Today* (February, 1983), 26-31.

a successful executive, interviewed the senior managers of several Fortune 500 corporations—the savvy insiders who had seen many people in the corporation come and go. In the course of the interviewing they learned that they could find out more by asking what derailed the promising people than by probing for the attributes of those who had climbed the corporate ladder successfully.

They compared twenty-one derailed executives with twenty who had "arrived." By the "derailed" they meant the promising people who were expected go higher in the organization but who plateaued in their careers, were fired, or were forced to retire early. The twenty "arrivers" were the people who made it all the way to the top. They discovered that the two groups were surprisingly alike: each had demonstrated remarkable strengths, and all were flawed by one or more significant weaknesses. That was their first discovery. Nobody was perfect; the derailers and the arrivers alike were a blending of lights and shadows.

Their second discovery had to do with the differences between the two groups when they put together the long list of limitations noted among the derailed. When these limitations are translated into their positive opposites, we can create a list of personal qualities and skills that characterize the top executives in business, on a scale of one to ten:

1. Sensitivity to others
2. Personal warmth and availability
3. Integrity
4. Loyalty (up, down and across the organization)
5. Superior overall business performance
6. Ability to delegate
7. Ability to build staff relationships
8. Ability to think strategically

9. Ability to adapt to superiors
10. Independence of spirit

Only two of the attributes are what might be called "executive job skills" with direct application to success in business, numbers five and eight. There is nothing here specifically about competence with budgets and balance sheets, nothing about marketing skills or predicting business trends or overseeing and adjusting profit margins. Some of the attributes are more *relational* than others, but all represent spiritual, emotional, and intellectual skills in using the power for participation—that is, in a collaborative or "looping" mode as opposed to the use of power in a competitive top-down or "linear" mode.

What this means is that business is much more an enterprise of soul than of cents, much more a matter of empowering people than of making money. Money remains critical: no profit, no business. But the high road to profit clearly follows the path of relationships. A business organization will succeed to the degree that it is in the hands of people skilled in the *unquantifiable* abilities of loyalty and integrity, attending to the needs of others, and working for the good of the whole. As one of the top senior executives told the researchers, "Only two things differentiated the successful from the derailed: total integrity, and understanding other people."

A striking correlation exists between what makes a successful leader and what employees in organizations really want. What this means is that the success of an executive relies on the intuitive match between the leader's gifts and the desires of those who are led. In the following research by the U. S.

Chamber of Commerce,[4] ten items of "worker desire" were rated in the left-hand column in their order of importance to the employees. In the right-hand column, those same items were ranked according to what employers *think* their employees want.

	Employee Ranking	Employer Ranking
Appreciation	1	8
Feeling "in" on things	2	10
Help with personal problems	3	9
Job security	4	2
Good wages	5	1
Interesting work	6	5
Promotions	7	3
Management loyalty to workers	8	6
Good working conditions	9	4
Tactful disciplining	10	7

Notice that the three *highest* values to employees—appreciation, feeling "in" on things, and help with personal problems—are the three *lowest* values employers assume are desirable to employees. On the other hand, the employers' perception of what the employees wanted—good wages, job security, and promotions—were only middle values for the employees. This discrepancy says at least two things of importance.

First, those who are led instinctively want the kind of leader who functions as a servant. Appreciation, inclusion, and concern for the well-being of others are values and expectations which only a relational style of leadership can be alert to—let alone fulfill. Second, the majority of leaders

---

4. The research was done in 1986 and reprinted in the *New Age Journal* in April, 1994.

have goals for their people that are woefully out of touch with the real hopes and needs of the people they lead. Whereas employers thought that money, job security, and upward mobility were the highest priorities for the people they employed, the workers themselves rated relationships far ahead of wages and promotions. Leaders need to be awakened to this reality, for their own sake and the sake of the companies they lead. Servant leadership is the foundation for success, the rock on which to build business achievement.

What the research suggests is that free-market capitalism, as it has evolved into profit-driven competitive consumerism, actually functions to *separate* leaders from the led. More than that, "capitalism as consumerism" separates all people from their own deepest personal needs. And yet it is possible to see signs of a transformation of capitalism taking place in businesses today. Often we can spot the leading edges of a major transition in cartoons. One by Dana Fradon printed in *The New Yorker* magazine in 1992 pictures a group of commuters awaiting their train into the city. Most are men suited out in coat, tie, and briefcase. Only two are women, one of them in furs and both fashionably hatted. All have their attention focused outward and upward, attending to the sky. Two of the men are in devotional postures of kneeling, another two are prostrate in worship. Fradon's caption reads: *"Corporate leaders gather in a field outside Darien, Connecticut, where one of them claims to have seen the Invisible Hand of the Marketplace."*[5] The power to expose free-market consumerism as idolatry—and thereby to de-legitimize it—can eventually redirect, or even bring down, a powerful and oppressive folly.

Every society develops around a dominant organizing myth, and ours is the idea that the economy should be para-

---

5. Dana Fradon, in *The New Yorker* (June 1992), 40.

mount, the institution around which everything revolves. Economic values control decisions. The mechanism for this decision-making is called "cost-benefit analysis," and it all seems so natural to us that it is nearly an act of treason to question it. The myth of "domination by the economy" rests on these basic assumptions:

- any organization must grow or die
- the economy as a whole must grow exponentially
- labor productivity must continue to increase
- owners have the right to receive the maximum return on their investments
- unbridled competition is a good thing, with a few minor exceptions.

But if we were to consider the goals that we *as a society* strive to fulfill, we might discover they are very different. Willis Harman, a scientist and educator, has summarized these societal goals in this way:

- we want a wholesome environment in which to raise our children
- we want a good relationship with nature
- we want to feel safe
- we hold dear certain values like democracy, liberty, the rule of law, equity, and justice.

Harman continues:

It turns out that if you look at the assumptions that underlie our economic system…and then you look at the goals we humans have about how we want to live our lives there is no compatibility. The assumptions can never lead to the goals. And yet this incompatibility passes unnoticed. I think that's because the assumptions about economic progress seemed to work rather well during the time when you could equate material progress with general benefit. But that equation doesn't work any more. We now have a system that works to the benefit of the few and penalizes masses of people today and into the future.[6]

Clearly, a fundamental transformation of the system is needed. The redirecting of capitalism has already begun in new and reformed business enterprises, including companies such as Ben and Jerry's Ice Cream in Vermont and Tom Chappell's personal products company, Tom's of Maine. These companies have designed and conducted their expressions of capitalism in ways that are congruent with the values that most human beings hold dear. And in both cases they became resounding business successes as they turned their corporate energies in the direction of serving individuals and the public good. Tom Chappell has written a book in which he recounts his own pilgrimage of turning away from consumer capitalism toward a more compassionate relationship with both people and the environment. In an interview Chappell described this journey:

> In my darkest days I was working for aims that were too narrow for me. I was working for market share, sales growth, and profits. It was a sense of emptiness. I was to some degree depressed, undirected, unconnected to myself. I felt like an actor because what I was doing was not authentic. I was a phony to myself because I wasn't living up to what I cared about. [The real thing is] not winning at all costs. It's challenging yourself to win according to who you are. So now I'm trying to engender more kind-

---

6. Willis Harman, "Transformation of Business," in the periodical *Yes,* vol. 41 (Summer, 1995), 52.

ness. I'm trying to link what I'm doing to the environment
and to the community.[7]

All across the social spectrum, in business and elsewhere,
people like Tom Chappell are reconnecting with their interior spirituality and transforming capitalism in the process.
They are developing businesses on the creative and restless
edges of the corporate world, like Tom's of Maine and Ben
and Jerry's Ice Cream. Parallels are emerging on the edges of
conventional religious settings, as in "house churches" that
seek to replicate the patterns of inclusion and outreaching
servanthood that mark the earliest Christian congregations.

Willis Harman was once asked how these new business
enterprises and spiritual movements would help bring about
the needed transformation of the whole economic system.
To answer, he used an analogy from biology that has to do
with the smooth way a caterpillar transforms itself into a
butterfly. As the "turning point" approaches certain kinds of
cells in the caterpillar's body begin to develop spontane-
ously. They appear to be responding to a "new vision" of life
for the creature. In biology these tiny body components are
called *imaginal* cells. Their work is to begin building the
various parts of the new organisms of the "envisioned" butterfly. As the new parts grow the tissue in between simply
gives way and disintegrates, in a very cooperative and non-
disruptive way. And lo, the caterpillar becomes a butterfly.

"I think something like this is happening in society,"
writes Harman, "with intentional communities, alternative
economies, alternative technology groups and all sorts of
movements and sub-movements....[These movements]
represent a whole side of ourselves that we had set aside in
our patriarchal society. Now they are emerging in force and

---

7. *Fortune* (December, 1994), 42.

creating all these little *imaginal* cells all over society. When the big structure comes down those cells will be there."[8]

Imaginal cells in business are growing steadily. Tom Chappell, in response to his sense of being disconnected from his true self as a business entrepreneur, decided on a part-time degree program in theology and ethics at the Harvard Divinity School. Not all such entrepreneurs go for a degree in theology, but all of them, in some personal way, respond to the impulses of the Spirit within them. I serve on the board of directors of two companies in Georgia led by people on the frontiers of business transformation. One of them, the industrial paint company in Macon, was cited in the previous chapter. The other is an automobile and truck dealership in Savannah employing about eighty men and women in the whole range of responsibilities related to selling and servicing fine vehicles. Both are experiencing new levels of company morale and profitability.

The leaders of imaginal business cells are marked by two fundamental attributes. First is their spiritual restlessness, their longing for a nobler aim in business than simply grinding out profits. Second is their commitment to see those with whom they work—their employees, customers, and suppliers—as real people who hunger for recognition and care, and to see the support of social and environmental realities as indispensable for their enterprises.

What these business cells prove is that spirituality and business belong together, even though superficially they can seem antithetical and perhaps even hostile to one another. The reason for this is full of irony. It goes back to origins of the world-view that made modern business possible—the philosophy of Descartes that laid the foundations of empirical science. Automatic transmissions and all the technolo-

---

8. Harman, "Transformation of Business," 54.

gies they represent are offsprings of the "clockworks" understanding of the cosmos encouraged by Cartesian philosophy, in which the universe is an inert collection of parts and pieces to be measured and manipulated into ever new forms for the convenience and profit of humankind. Francis Bacon talked about the work of science as "torturing nature's secrets from her," using the analogy of burning secrets from the witches whom the king sent to the stake. There can be no doubt about the accomplishments of the old science, but its bounty has become a double-edged sword. While stimulating human ingenuity it has also alienated matter from spirit. *What can be counted is the only thing that counts.* What can be measured is the only thing that has any real importance—in business and the world of hard reality. If what can be counted is the only thing that counts, how can we resist the attraction of profits since, in business, operational profits and losses are the one thing that can be accurately counted? If the "measurable" is the only dependable measurement of business success, why worry about the immeasurable?

∞

I once invited a communicant in the Diocese of Atlanta who was chairman and CEO of a large and profitable corporation to send one of his senior executives to test our newly created seminars in servant leadership under the joint sponsorship of the schools of theology and business administration at Emory University. He responded with a tart question: "What makes you think this corporation has anything to learn from Sunday school?" He was not a cynical man, and was keenly devoted to values of family and his church. But for him the separation of matter and spirit into air-tight, separate categories was as clear as the split between tin pans and poetry.

This is the inner legacy of "reductionist" science, the materialist view of reality that, by reducing matter to its lowest level of constituent parts, has invented machines and laid the groundwork for the technology that commands today's commerce. Three centuries of the human pilgrimage have been dominated by the idea that the material order commands a higher human interest and legitimacy than the spiritual. Calculation and computation lie at the foundation of business success; all else is optional, perhaps even unimportant. The "bottom line" has become the preoccupation and passion of conventional business. Little wonder that my Atlanta communicant, whose Christian allegiance was formed by a religious tradition that long ago abdicated the world of hard reality to science and economics, would feel uncomfortable with the notion that business and spirituality belong together.

Religion seems to have been similarly seduced. As business has come to consist of *profits*, religion has tended to consist of *propositions* that we call dogma. The left-brain functions of empirical measurement and analysis have tended to command the theological field, while the right-brain functions of intuition and passion are distrusted. Enchanted for generations by a mechanistic view of reality, both the institutions of commercial enterprise and the institutions of religion have been kept apart by misperceptions of one another—and perhaps even misperceptions of themselves.

When people are asked to tell about their moments of inner awakening and a sense of encounter with God, more than half of these will have occurred in unexpected places: on a street car in Honolulu at the close of World War II, on a beach at twilight, on hearing a concerto by a virtuoso cellist, on holding a newborn child. Some of these moments happen under plainly religious auspices, possibly at a church camp or retreat—maybe even during a sermon. But always these moments, whether in church or not, are better remembered for the sensations they aroused than for what was heard. These are intuitive experiences, precisely in accord with scripture, where God is met far more often in the world than in the sanctuary. Elijah heard the "sound of gentle stillness" at the mouth of a cave. Jesus caught the voice of his Father as he came up from his baptismal dip in a muddy river. Saul of Tarsus was thrown to the road on his way to Damascus and was never the same.

If you ask any dozen churchgoers to tell about their faith, it is likely that no one will repeat the Nicene Creed, even though in most mainline churches this theological statement is said aloud nearly every Sunday. While organized religion does require conceptual clarity in its defining articles of faith, its real hold on people is not intellectual. It is personal and experiential. The energy of worship is passion, not proposition. Spirituality and religion are related but not identical. Religion needs dogma, structure, and left-brain definition in creeds and ritual for its own continuity; spirituality is the impulse of every human heart searching for meaning and courage in life's journey. If it is true that spirituality is essentially intuitive and relational, then the *connection* between business and spirituality becomes vivid and real, because the terms that define the real activity of business are fluid and evolving—terms like marketing, motivating, inventing, designing, forecasting, training, collaborating, competing.

These words blend computation and conjecture, left-brain and right-brain, with far heavier reliance on intuition and imagination. Right-brain activity represents the fundamental disequilibrium of life, its resistance to being nailed down securely in quantitative terms, its insistence on a capacity of the spirit to adjust and change in response to the unexpected. And spirituality itself is life in disequilibrium, a readiness to relinquish tight control and yield oneself in trust and love to God, however God is known. Albert Einstein intuited his theory of relativity long before he could demonstrate its dynamics in the formula $E=MC^2$. I am told that his theory came to him after a long stretch of lying sick in bed, during which he asked himself, "What would the world look like if I rode a beam of light?" Doubtless it was his reliance on this kind of inventive imagining that led him to say of himself later in life, "When I examine myself and my methods of thought, I come to the conclusion that the gift of fantasy has meant far more to me than my talent for absorbing positive knowledge."

The old science alienated business from spirituality by assuming hard regularity and predictability in the natural order, assumptions that the new science has disproved. Postmodern scientists know that the cosmos is not a machine. Rather, it is a system pulsing with life and ultimate mystery. Nor are business enterprises machines, but networks of living relationships in an adventure of ceaseless search. There is a large element of mastery in cost-control, but most of the real energy that sustains a business—like the energy that sustains the cosmos—is in the realm of mystery, in hunches and hopes, in relationships of trust and expectation invested in the people who will make or break the business.

So we turn now to this new science, and the foundation that it lays for servant leadership in the world through its new conception of a "relational" approach to power.

Chapter 9

Servanthood and Science

The two most powerful forces in human history are science and religion. The future of humanity depends now more than anything else on how these two forces settle down in relation to one another.

—Alfred North Whitehead

My generation was taught to think of the universe as "matter in motion." The structure of the cosmos was governed entirely by mechanical laws. Predictability and regularity made science and technology possible, for the cosmos itself was literally a machine. Rene Descartes developed this image of a cosmic machine from a dream that came to him in 1619. The universe, he decided, is like the workings of a clock, and by applying mathematical principles to the atomic structure of "things" nature could be researched, manipulated, and rearranged for human convenience and profit.

In 1687 Isaac Newton summed up the laws of universal mechanics in a series of algebraic formulations. The long-term effect of Newton's work on the scientific community was to reduce the "mystery" of the universe to a confidence in human "mastery." The cosmos was packed into a neat box, where it remained for nearly three hundred years. Both Descartes and Newton taught that atoms were the basic building blocks of the cosmos and that they floated in a void, "on their own," without any connectivity or community. Relationship was only incidental—or perhaps ornamental, as in the interaction and flow of colors in works of art.

This paradigm functioned so persuasively that it has created the most powerful base of knowledge the world has ever known. Charles Darwin's work the *Origin of Species* gave further impetus to the "atomization" of all aspects of life. Families, education, business, nation-states, religion, sports—most departments of human experience have come to reflect the supreme value of the separate individual.

Nowhere is the influence of an atomized world-view more powerful than in the realm of economics. In matters of money. The seductive engine of human striving called "competition" has utterly eclipsed cooperation and collaboration on the scale of popular values. In 1889 Andrew Carnegie published an essay categorically denying that the Christian religion has anything to say about how money is made. Instead, he insisted that the production of wealth is governed by competition of tooth and fang, the Darwinian laws of survival of the fittest. Carnegie went on to maintain that "these laws of survival account for the uneven acquisition of wealth and *fully justify* the wide discrepancy between the rich and the poor."[1]

Some brave and prophetic souls took exception. In his second Inaugural Address in 1936, for example, Franklin Roosevelt spoke for the victims of heartless individualism:

---

1. M. Douglas Meeks, *God the Economist* (Minneapolis: Fortress Press, 1989), 21. Italics mine.

> We have always known that heedless self-interest was
> bad morals; we know now that it is bad economics....The
> test of our progress is not whether we add more to the
> abundance of those who have much; it is whether we
> provide for those who have too little.

Roosevelt's moral protest of the "atomization" of life was
echoed in the scientific research of two of his contemporar-
ies. The old cosmology, which glorified the individual and
exalted competition as the driving social and economic
value, began to unravel with the work of Albert Einstein and
the Danish physicist Neils Bohr. They discovered that it is
impossible to pin down the elusive and intricate behavior of
atoms, and that atoms themselves are not the last word in
the structure of physical reality. Crowding the so-called
physical world, below the level of the atom, are subatomic
particles or waves of harmonic resonances that behave with
"unscientific abandon." The new cosmology knows that atoms are intricately complex and interwoven, composed of
smaller particles with names like "quarks" and "sub-quarks"
that elude precise observation. Moreover, light particles
(photons) behave like cars on an interstate; that is, most will
follow a predictable path of traveling steadily forward while
some will veer off, as if taking an exit ramp. And it is impossible to predict which photons will travel on and which will
exit.

Einstein and Bohr resisted these discoveries and deduc-
tions for as long they could, since they opened the once-tidy
world to a vast untidiness and confusion that science now
calls "chaos." The further they took their investigations, the
more the untidiness revealed a mystical relatedness that
operates both predictably and randomly—exactly like people. The cosmos now seems to be a living body in which no
part behaves independently from any other. Lately we have

come to realize that two particles separated by whole galaxies somehow *know* what the other is doing. If we change the spin on one particle, the other reverses its spin wherever it is, instantaneously, using some form of communication faster than light.

The meteorologist Edward Lorenz, puzzled by his inability to forecast weather with precision, developed what he calls the "butterfly effect" because he found that all weather patterns are sensitive to the prevailing conditions of other weather patterns. Everything is connected to everything else: when a butterfly beats its wings in Tokyo, it ultimately affects the weather in New York. This is one expression of "chaos theory." It sounds as if the cosmos is out of control, but it is not. The cosmos is like people, who are better known for their behavior than for their chemical composition. Even our chemistry is more a matter of behavior than a collection of atomic particles. At the subatomic level chemicals behave exactly like people—both predictably and unpredictably—from babies in the crib to athletes competing on playing fields. The point of chaos theory is that there is an order to cosmic ardor. Chaos operates within boundaries that correspond to the sides of the baby's crib or to the out-of-bounds on the football field, but within those wide boundaries there are no observers, only participants. Nobody is "on" the earth as an object; every living entity is "in" the earth as a subject—as part of a vast, pulsing, interwoven web of life.

This new science radically changes the way we see the world. *Relationship is the key to the cosmos.* This new view of the world will increasingly change the way we structure all of life's interactions—in business, politics, education, the church, and in every organized enterprise. Nowhere are the changes more apparent than in the character of the nations in their relationships with one another, where violence must increasingly be repudiated in favor of patient and painful diplomacy. Most of the world is united in its condemnation of the carnage in the Serbian-Bosnian war, and the hesitancy of the nations to escalate the violence by military intervention reflect a growing antipathy to using war as a problem-solver.

The new vision comes in the nick of time. Walter Brueggemann, the biblical scholar, offers a proverb for our time: "The world for which you have been so carefully prepared is being taken away from you, *by the grace of God.*"[2] Not only is the cosmos profoundly relational, the life and health of that awesome interwovenness is anchored in its diversity. Biologists now know that when the exuberance of diversity is reduced vitality goes with it—when enough is subtracted, life itself becomes dysfunctional and collapses, tumbling in on itself.

Gary Zukav, not himself a physicist but an adventurer at the frontiers of human knowing, wrote a book about the new physics after an experience of getting to know quantum theorists. In his introduction he wrote that a friend had invited him to an afternoon conference at the Lawrence Berkeley Laboratory in California some years before. "At that time I had no connections with the scientific community, so I went to see what physicists were like. To my great surprise, I discovered that (1) I understood everything they said, and (2) their discussion sounded very much like a theological discussion."[3]

Brian Swimme, an American astrophysicist, notes that we used to call the bonding energy that holds the cosmos to-

---

2. Quoted by Barbara Brown Taylor in "Preaching into the Third Millennium," an essay in the *Journal for Preachers*, vol. 19, no. 3 (Easter 1996), 25-31.

3. Gary Zukav, *The Dancing Wui Li Masters* (New York: Bantam Books, 1979), xvii.

gether "gravity" and "electromagnetism." These are still good words but no longer good enough in the light of the new physics. The more we know about the universe, he continues, the more we want to use feeling words like "affection" and "intimacy." What this means is that the bonding ingredient in the new cosmology is *love*. The conceptual embrace of quantum science now includes the spirit of caring—a love that includes the energies of mercy and forgiveness in order that broken relationships may be restored. "No two particles [in the universe] can be considered disconnected, ever," Swimme concludes.[4]

Quantum physicists talk more and more like theologians, even on matters of sin. Again, Brian Swimme:

> The loss of relationship, with its consequent alienation, is a kind of supreme evil in the universe. In the religious world this was traditionally understood as an ultimate mystery. To be locked up in a private world, to be cut off from intimacy with other beings, to be incapable of entering the joy of mutual presence—such conditions were taken as the essence of damnation.[5]

Love is what everything is reaching for, at all levels of the cosmos. Exploitation will compel withdrawal, from the largest to the smallest entity, from the most conscious to the most unreflective, from one's wife or husband to the dog and the cat—even to machines and appliances. Neglect and exploit your lawnmower and it will eventually withdraw, freeze up, disintegrate. But love for anything, with appropriate care and honor, will nurture relationships (including the atoms in a machine) and make life flourish—especially when per-

---

4. Brian Swimme and Thomas Berry, *The Universe Story* (San Francisco: HarperCollins, 1992), 78.

5. *Ibid.*

sonal responsibility is insisted upon and we are held accountable for our behavior.

It appears that we intuitively knew this long ago. Before Descartes and Newton, an Anglican theologian told the same "universe story" that Brian Swimme and Thomas Berry now tell as scientists. Richard Hooker, preaching on pride, told his congregation:

> God hath created nothing simply for itself: but each thing in all things, and everything in each part in other hath such interest, that in the whole world nothing is found whereunto anything created can say, "I need thee not."

Compare Hooker's theology to the latest research of post-modern science:

> Existence itself is derived from and sustained by this intimacy of each being with every other being in the universe....Indeed the earth is so integral in the unity of its functioning that...the well-being of the planet is a condition for the well-being of any of the component members of the planetary community. To preserve the economic viability of the planet must be the first law of economics. To preserve the health of the planet must be the first law of the medical profession. To preserve the natural world as the primary revelation of the divine must be the basic concern of religion....The well-being of the earth is primary. Human well-being is derivative.[6]

Physics is now reminding religion of what we have known all along: that the created place of humanity in the divine order of things is *derivative*. "The Lord God formed a human being from the dust of the ground and breathed into his nostrils the

---

6. *Ibid.*, 278.

breath of life, so that he became a living creature" (Genesis 2:7, REB).

∽

The "new" cosmology is accompanied by a fresh epistemology, a new approach to learning that seeks to answer the question, "How can we arrive at dependable knowledge?" Most of us have been taught an approach to knowledge that discounts any reliance on the spirit—any intrusion of the "subjective" into strict "objective" observation. In this approach relational knowing is inferior and undependable. Truly dependable knowledge consists only of what can be reduced to quantification. The "truth" can therefore be known only from what will yield to precise objective measurement.

The philosophical term for this approach to knowing is "reductionism." It implies that the only access to real knowledge comes from breaking matter down to its constituent parts, separated from its connections to other parts and from the scientific observer. Any involvement with the investigator lessens dependability; the researcher must stay at a distance so as not to distort the purity of results. Feelings cannot enter into scientific processes since the only things that count are what can be counted. Such an approach to knowledge is the reverse of a "relational" understanding of truth. Spirit is out of bounds, and *this is the foundation of the long-standing divorce of science from religion.*

No doubt the divorce had to come. The pre-Copernican religious establishment of Europe held investigative science in contempt and frequently persecuted its pioneers, like Galileo. So science was forced to go its own way. By now, however, what was daring and new in the sixteenth and seventeenth centuries is old, even lethal. Its epistemology has become dangerously obsolete, made so by the very methods of empirical investigation that brought on the divorce of science and religion. For this kind of science, that science itself has made old, the highest form of knowledge consisted of grasping objects in all their conceptual purity. This is the source of Francis Bacon's famous dictum, "knowledge is power." The grasper of objective facts becomes the master of objectified nature. Empirical science can thus grasp and even rearrange the natural order to human advantage. And the reason that the old epistemology held sway for three hundred years is that it succeeded extravagantly well in its goal of rearranging life to human convenience and material wealth. The success of knowledge as power is epitomized by the slogan: "Don't Be a Dishwasher, Buy One!"

A new epistemology has now been birthed by science itself: empirical and relational knowers march together, often in the same person. Parker Palmer tells the true story of Barbara McClintock, a geneticist who died recently. As a young biologist she became enthralled with the puzzle of genetic transmission. She pursued hypotheses that seemed so outrageous to conventional science that she could find no grants for research, no fellowships, not even lab space—until in her early eighties she was recognized for unique and original achievement and was awarded a Nobel Prize. Because of her unfashionable approach to scientific investigation, she had to use the cheapest available research material: field corn. All her life McClintock toiled on ears of corn. When asked how this kind of science was done, she replied, "You have to have a feel for the organism." Not satisfied that this was an adequate scientific response, her interviewer pressed her further. "Now really, how is this kind of intricate research done?" After some thought, McClintock answered, "I guess the only way to put it is to say that you must learn to *lean into the ear of corn.*"

By this McClintock does not mean the absence of hard facts and figures, or their neglect in serious scientific research. She is saying that "factoring" and "feeling" are partners in the search for knowledge—that measurement and mystery belong together. Computation and intuition serve one another, and the highest science is one that depends on "relational" knowing.

Consider what this can mean to the work of servant leadership. Postmodern science is clear that the most "scientific management" is *fundamentally relational*—and never precisely measurable. This is only to ratify what we have always known deep down: that the most dependable knowledge-base on which to build effective leadership is firmly anchored in the realm of the spirit. McClintock's biographer said of her what ought to be a benchmark by which to identify a servant leader: "Dr. McClintock, in her relationship with corn, achieved the highest from of love, which is *intimacy that does not destroy difference.*"[7]

If it is true that "fear" and "love" are the two basic human responses to life—and I believe they are—then objectivity carries with it a hidden component of fear. It denies the power of the material that is being studied to affect the student deeply. It denies the power of the led to influence the leader. It is blind to the power of those who are taught to teach the teacher. In simplest terms, the epistemology of objectivity is *fearful of losing control.* At its core, objectivism will not risk the enrichment that comes of not just *grasping* knowledge, but also of *being grasped* by it and thereby being transformed. This is the mystical ingredient in a relational epistemology: the thrill of being grasped by what you seek to

---

7. Evelyn Fox Keller, quoted in Parker J. Palmer, "The Great Conversation," a taped lecture given at the Trinity Institute in New York in 1993.

grasp. It is the hidden reward in a posture of openness to the "other." It is riskier but richer. It is an experience of the way power works in the universe—always as an exchange, moving back and forth and around a dynamic circle of relationships.

This is clearly the emerging world-view—a view of the world become too small for violence and too precious for plunder. Albert Einstein captured the essence of servanthood and the new science in a single paragraph of great truth and beauty:

> A human being is part of the whole, of what we call the universe, a part limited in time and space. We experience ourselves, our thoughts and feelings, as something separate from the rest. This is a kind of optical illusion of consciousness. This illusion is a kind of prison for us, restricting us to our personal desires and to affection for those closest to us. Our task must be to free ourselves from this prison by widening our circle of compassion for all living creatures and the whole of nature in its beauty.

Chapter 10

Servanthood and the Environment

We travel together, passengers on a little spaceship, dependent on its vulnerable supplies of air and soil; all committed for our safety to its security and peace, preserved from annihilation only by the care, the work, and I will say, the love we give our fragile craft.

—Adlai E. Stevenson

Adlai Stevenson was among the first of the world's political leaders to awaken to the perils of the planet and to call the nations to make changes in their perception and behavior toward the environment. His warning about the need to care for the "fragile craft" on which we all dwell was part of the last address he delivered as the U. S. Ambassador to the United Nations, given before a world assembly of decision-makers in Geneva, Switzerland on July 9, 1965, only a few days before he died.

Does our Christian allegiance make room for Stevenson's tender affirmation to "love" the earth? Can a person with a passion for preserving the earth maintain a detachment from the earth that distinguishes nature from nature's God?

Is it possible to love both God and the planet without confusing the two, and so avoid sliding into a pantheism that worships creation as its own creator? If it is possible for an orthodox Christian to cherish the planet and work for its preservation, why then does the religious community appear so indifferent to the environmental movement? If Judaism and Christianity make room for a public shift from earth-plunder to earth-care, why does organized religion regard the issue as peripheral? There are, of course, some conspicuous exceptions: here and there a few local congregations and national church commissions are paying attention to the global environment. But on the whole the mounting threat to creation is not on the religious agenda.

Care for the earth fuels almost exclusively the concern of secular agencies like Greenpeace, the Nature Conservancy, Friends of the Earth, and the World-Watch Institute. Yet these agencies are dismissed and sometimes vilified by political and industrial leaders who go regularly to church. The late Carl Sagan had to plead with the religious community to get involved, saying at the North American Conference on Religion and the Environment in Washington, D. C. in 1990, "Technology alone cannot handle the peril to the earth. We in the scientific community can help, and we must, but to apply technology without moral and spiritual undergirding is only to compound the problem, because most of the roots of the crisis lie deep in a heedless technological fever."

Why should the religious community have to be exhorted by contemporary scientists to attend to the earth when the Judeo-Christian scriptures are anchored in the creation story from the beginning? Ironically, the biblical creation story itself can be the very source of religious detachment. The Israelites differed sharply in their world-view from the tribes of Baal worshipers who surrounded them and whom they later displaced in the land. For the Canaanites, nature was shot through with the gods of nature: fertility gods, the gods of sun and moon, of wind and rain. For them nature itself was divine. By contrast, the Israelites did not regard nature as sacred for *being* divine; nature participated in sacredness by *belonging* to divinity, owned by nature's divine Creator—as a log house in the wilderness is the possession of its builder. "The heavens are yours, the earth is also yours; the world and all that is in it—you have founded them" (Psalm 89:11).

This is the basic separation of Creator from creation that lies at the roots of our Judeo-Christian tradition. The Bible is a document of disenchantment. Whereas pagan spirituality made no sharp distinction between the natural and divine orders, our religious forbears experienced the divine as the transcendent author of all that is. "In the beginning when God created the heavens and the earth..." (Genesis 1:1). The Israelites knew themselves as separate from the natural order, made in the image of the transcendent God. Yet scripture not only sets humankind apart in the image of God, it gives us the vocation of domination as rulers and subduers of the earth. That is one of the reasons for developing a "natural" sense of superiority over nature. Human beings are "on" the earth as ruling subjects; all other things are "in" nature as objects to be ruled. "God said to them, 'Be fruitful and multiply, and fill the earth and subdue it; and have dominion over the fish of the sea and over the birds of the air and over every living thing that moves upon the earth'" (Genesis 1:28). On the face of it this passage is a divine manifesto for human control and, eventually, heedless plunder of the natural order.

The founders of modern science—Copernicus, Galileo, Descartes, and Newton—all professed and practiced an earnest Christian faith. All were shaped by the scriptural mandate to take dominion and subdue the earth. Small wonder therefore that we think of ourselves as manipulators of nature, developing industries and economies that advance "dominion" of the earth to the extremities of exploitation and plunder in our search for material prosperity. Obviously this is not the only reason for religious indifference to the environmental crisis, but it seems basic. Our radical separation from our roots in the seas and soils can be traced back to the ways we have understood—or misunderstood—the commands and promises of the Genesis story.

The plea of this chapter is that we seize our vocation of stewardship of the earth as a divine calling, that we learn to care for creation as servant leaders. The need for a servanthood to creation is overwhelming. The World-Watch Institute estimates that just before Adlai Stevenson made his plea to love the earth the capacity of the earth to replenish itself as a life-support system was over-reached. In 1956 the earth passed the point of self-renewal. More than forty years ago the earth began a slow but accelerating diminishment of its resource-renewing energies. Only six percent of the world's forest has any official protection, and at current rates we will denude the planet within two or three generations—though the rising demand for farmland and wood products and the accelerating global trade threaten to increase that rate.[1] Other ominous elements of the environmental crisis are well known: the degradation of the seas and soils, and the rising threat of global warming. There is less need to detail the perils than to sound a hopeful note and encourage participation as servant leaders in turning things around before it is too late.

---

1. *World-Watch*, vol. 10, no. 1 (January/February, 1997), 42.

∞

Three fundamental insights are necessary in order for servant leaders to serve the earth. The first is the need to reconcile scientific and religious assumptions about creation. The second is to come to a deeper meaning of the biblical story of creation and human stewardship, while the third is the need to press for political actions that will change the way nations, businesses, and individuals use the earth's resources.

In his book *Global Mind Change*, physicist Willis Harman poignantly describes the beginning of the reunion of science and religion:

> The modern world long assumed that there was a fundamental incompatibility between science and religion. For a time it appeared as a series of direct conflicts over such issues as the age of the earth, the meaning of fossil records, and evolutionary theory. Then as the world moved well into the twentieth century the conflict subsided, and people tended to live their religious lives apart from whatever they thought science was telling them about reality. The price paid for this schizophrenia was that neither science nor religion fully satisfied the [inner] desire to *know*.[2]

Harman goes on to say that scientific assumptions have now moved far beyond the earlier view that "spirit emerged from matter," as if "matter" were the fundamental stuff of the universe. As pointed out in the preceding chapter, most advanced scientific inquiry today sees "spirit" as the ultimate

---

2.   Willis W. Harman, *Global Mind Change* (Indianapolis: Knowledge Systems, Inc., 1988), 82.

stuff of the universe. Consciousness is no longer understood as the end-product of the evolutionary process; it is the beginning. Matter does not create spirit; spirit creates matter. Religion and science agree: *consciousness precedes being in the creation of the universe.*

This is precisely what Teilhard de Chardin was claiming in the 1930s when he wrote that "molecules make love." In creation there is a preexistent love to which the material order awakens—from the tiniest cosmic ingredient to the self-reflective consciousness in humanity.

So there is no apparent reason for a conflict between what Harman calls a "mature" science and a "mature" religion. "Indeed," says Harman, "we must seriously question whether we have a mature science as long as such a conflict appears to exist."[3] If science makes no room for faith and prayer, the immaturity is in science, not in religion. These convictions of a physicist are echoed by the equally strong views of the theologian Jürgen Moltmann:

> In a global situation where it is the case of "one world or none" science and theology cannot afford to divide up the one, single reality. On the contrary, theology and the sciences will arrive together at the ecological awareness of the world.[4]

The second environmental insight for servant leaders rises from a deeper understanding of the critical Genesis passage. When the key words in English, "subdue" and "dominion," are understood in the original Hebrew, they convey radically (meaning "at the root") different meanings. The Hebrew for subdue is *kabash;* for dominion it is *radah.*

---

3. *Ibid.,* 104.

4. Jürgen Moltmann, *God in Creation* (San Francisco: HarperCollins, 1991).

Kabash translated as subdue implies that the earth is a hostile counterforce that humanity is divinely authorized to contain and enslave. Yet *kabash* in Hebrew is an agricultural term that means "to cultivate," "to prepare for planting." It implies cooperation with forces that are for us, not against us. In this reading "subdue" means to release the waiting powers of nature, powers within nature designed by God for nourishment in life. "Subdue" means to release, not to conquer—to cooperate with God as co-creators.

This view is the source of what is called "depth ecology"—humanity as rooted in the land and dependent on its waters. This perception gives the environmental movement a vital dimension of spirituality, moving the human spirit to levels far more profound than self-preserving economics. It gives economics a foundation of *abundance* in contrast to the conventional and competitive perception of *scarcity*. Depth ecology becomes a servanthood to the mothering earth. It takes Jesus seriously in his promise that in seeking God's kingdom and God's justice all needful things will be ours: "But if God so clothes the grass of the field...will he not much more clothe you?" (Matthew 6:30).

Depth ecology comes down to this: the unfailing energy of the universe is love. All things move to the mystical impulse of love. This is why beans will yield more beans to the gardener who "subdues" the garden in servanthood. Exploitation prompts withdrawal, but serving the living soil blesses both the seeds and the sower because the universe is built for loving. Postmodern science understands this kinship of all life: "molecules make love," or die for want of it.

The reason things work this way is implicit in the meaning of the second charge of God to Adam in the creation story, who is commissioned to take "dominion" over every living thing on the earth. In current usage "dominion" means "to control," but this is far from the meaning of the original, *radah,* which means in Hebrew "to rule as God rules." So the question becomes, "How does God rule?" Does God oppress or liberate, imprison or release? Does God rule in self-aggrandizement or in self-giving? Is divine sovereignty principally jealous or merciful? Is God's glory in the face of Jesus Christ a parade of conquering might or a compassionate and suffering servanthood? Are the divine laws that rule the cosmos meant to restrict or to instruct? And when the commandments are violated, what then?

Scripture has much to say about God's rule. During Israel's exile the prophet Isaiah spoke of the mercy of God:

> Let the wicked forsake their way,
>   and the unrighteous their thoughts;
> let them return to the Lord,
>   that he may have mercy on them,
> and to our God, for he will abundantly pardon.
>
> (Isaiah 55:7)

And much earlier in the story of God's dealings with the people of Israel there appears a rainbow of overarching compassion:

> Then God said to Noah,..."I am establishing my covenant with you and your descendants after you, and with every living creature that is with you, the birds, the domestic animals, and every animal of the earth with you, as many as came out of the ark. I establish my covenant with you, that never again shall all flesh be cut off by the waters of a flood, and never again shall there be a flood to destroy the earth....As long as the earth endures, seedtime and harvest, cold and heat, summer and winter, day and night, shall not cease." (Genesis 9:8-11, 8:22)

What do these passages tell us about the character of divine rule? *First,* it is gracious; supportive and not punitive.

Vengeful destruction will never again be an expression of God's power to rule. If demolition is no longer an option in God's rule, then what are the consequences of violating that dominion? In a structure of moral order is there no retribution for moral disorder?

It is the character of love to be more focused on the beloved than on itself. This means that "ruling as God rules" will always seek the good of the ruled, never their destruction. Consequences always attend violation, but these consequences are felt more by the ruler than the ruled. This is the meaning of the cross in the Christian tradition; the suffering of love is central to the theology of servanthood. God assumes the cost of grace in forgiveness, and because love *of* humanity demands freedom *for* humanity, grace cannot interfere with the human freedom *not* to love.

Parallel to this costly grace of God's dominion is the reality that punishment and reward are built into the moral order, and they are the inescapable consequences of moral freedom. It is precisely the retributive justice in God's dominion that brings about the degradation of the planet when we use our freedom to exploit and abuse the gift of creation. Jesus' story of the forgiving father and his two sons is the enduring statement of truth in a gracious universe (Luke 15:11-32). The father, as the suffering servant, runs out to greet the penitent younger son, not waiting for him to knock on the door. The younger son, having suffered the consequences of freedom misused in riotous living, resolves to return in penitence and admit his mistakes. "Father, I have sinned;...treat me like one of your hired hands." "Quickly, bring out a robe—the best one—and put it on him," the father orders in reply. Grace abounds in response to truth declared and responsibility assumed. But the older brother, unaware of the graciousness of his father's dominion, is the one most punished in a universe of love—punished by his own refusal of grace and his angry alienation from the family.

The _second_ thing the scriptures tell us is that God's rule is lavishly inclusive. All the animals enter the ark, and Noah and his handful of relatives are commissioned to a permanent stewardship of the earth. Thus "dominion" in human terms means serving creation in all its abundance. In this reading of scripture God's bestowal of dominion over creation cannot mean human ownership and abuse. It means costly care.

In January, 1962 my wife and I sailed on another ark with our three young children, a modern ship, the _President Cleveland,_ bound for Yokohama from San Francisco. I was on assignment as an interim missionary for six months to an English-speaking congregation of Anglicans in Tokyo. Most were American and British, involved in business, the military, and the diplomatic corps. A few were Australians and New Zealanders. Some were from China, Taiwan, India, and Ceylon (now Sri Lanka), and several of the usual hundred or so communicants on a Sunday morning were Japanese— some of them Christian, others Shinto/Buddhist inquirers.

Soon after we arrived John Glenn traveled around the planet on February 20, 1962 and took the first snapshots of our round earth from space with, to the delight of the Japanese, a Minolta camera. We had come to Japan in awe of the size of the earth: it had taken us ten days to come less than halfway around the world. As we had entered Tokyo Bay in the dawn light we could see the snows of Mount Fuji fifty miles distant, and I had felt overwhelmed by how far we were from Baltimore and home. By the time we returned to Baltimore ten months later, having sailed around the world by two more steamships and a few trains through Europe, the planet had shrunk almost to the size of a neighborhood. Everywhere we went English was spoken and John Kennedy and Pope John XXIII were heroes to half the world. It no longer seemed incredible that John Glenn had circled the earth three times in less than five hours, at 17,545 miles an hour. We had left home seeing the world as immensely big and its people few; we returned home seeing the world as small and its people many.

Everyone operates from their own perspective on the world. From where I live, it is a crowded neighborhood. But when I see the world from the perspective of the forests of the Pacific Northwest or the agricultural fields of the Midwest, the world looks spacious and indestructible. There the environment appears subordinate to the economy, and production looks like the making of things to meet the rising appetite of humans for food, paper products, cars, and airplanes. This prevailing world-view is familiar and comforting, but it is demonstrably false. A world that is organized and operated by the appetites of "growth economies" is unsustainable.

One way to address these voracious appetites is to create a new tax system that would shift gradually from taxing income to taxing the use of depleting resources—because what is taxed now through the earnings of people and corporations is ultimately tied to what the earth supplies in the form of biological diversity, soil, water, air, trees, oil, and minerals. As these resources diminish, the earnings tax base also diminishes. By simple extrapolation it is easy to see that, looking down the prevailing world-view road, not only will the resource base collapse, but the money supply with it. Taxes are not the enemy. It is the *tax base* that penalizes wage earners while subsidizing a bloated weapons industry, the below-market sales of public timber, and scarce public water for irrigation. World-Watch researcher Alan Durning has noted:

Taxes work at cross-purposes with public aims. Taxes penalize enterprise and investment; aggravate inequality; and accelerate environmental decline. They give the wrong incentives to almost everyone. They are, to borrow a phrase from energy analyst Amory Lovins, "spherically senseless"—no matter how you look at them they are nonsense.[5]

This wisdom has already been recognized in some places. In some parts of Europe, for example, taxation bases have begun to reflect a sensitivity to the perishing resources of the earth. Six nations of Europe have lowered income taxes and raised government revenues on environmental usage: Norway, Sweden, Denmark, Finland, Spain, and the United Kingdom. Imagine what might happen in the American presidential campaign in the year 2000 if an aspirant for the office should come out strongly for a significant reduction of military, industrial, and agricultural subsidies, along with a graduated boost in gasoline and fuel oil taxes, and parallel reductions in income taxes, especially for the lower and middle range wage earners. Could such a candidate be elected? Probably not. Attitudes do not change that fast. But somewhere within the early years of the next millennium the United States will join the European nations in taxing environmental depletion.

This brings us to the *third* fundamental insight required of servant leadership to the environment: to embrace a realistic world-view that cherishes the earth and to press political and economic leaders toward the wise and loving use of its resources. The task can seem overwhelming, but every action, no matter how small, contributes to a proper stewardship of the earth. Already we recycle so well in Henderson

---

5. *World-Watch*, 29.

County, North Carolina, for example, that projected increases in landfill availability have been postponed! Let no one think of recycling as a shallow response to the earth crisis. It is fundamental in two ways. First, it exactly reflects the divine economy of creation: the planet is a system of recovering and reusing its own resources. Second, recycling is the cornerstone of a momentous shift in human economics—from heedless extraction to planned restoration.

It may help to know that ours is not the first generation of servant leaders to awaken to the folly of human indifference toward the earth. St. Basil, Bishop of Caesarea, wrote the following prayer in the fourth century:

> O God, enlarge within us the sense of fellowship with all living things, our brothers the animals to whom thou gavest the earth in common with us....We remember with shame that in the past we have exercised the high dominion of man with ruthless cruelty, so that the voice of the earth, which should have gone up to thee in song, has been a groan of travail. We realize that they, the earth's creatures, live not alone for us, but for themselves and thee—and that they too love the sweetness of life.

To despair of the future is to discount human nobility and creativity, and to underrate the capacity of the human spirit to respond to every crisis.

Despair of the future is not only unfair to our children, it is out of touch with what children are thinking and hoping today. During the presidential election season of 1996, the small daily paper in Hendersonville, North Carolina, asked the local school children to write a brief statement that began "If I were president...." Here is what one of them wrote.

> Hi, I'm Samantha Young. You could call me Sam. I hope to be president of the United States. I would make a rule

about no fighting. Please elect me so we can clean the
Earth up....I would stop all wars and help all people,
especially the poor. I would change doctor bills by making them cheaper. All races black or white would be
treated the same....Children could vote for president. All
the guns will be melted down in our world.

I hope Samantha stays young! Her child's heart charts the
saving course for the human odyssey in the third millennium. Already at age nine she dares the dreams of a servant
leader: she pleads the cause of care for the earth, she urges
compassion and justice for all kinds and conditions of the
earth's people, and she knows the world's vast need of nonviolence. It is to the meaning and practice of nonviolence
that we turn in the chapter that follows.

Chapter 11

Servanthood as Nonviolence

Everyone knows that Christianity is a religion of nonviolence except the Christians.

—Mohandas K. Gandhi

What we call servant leadership, Gandhi called *satyagraha*. In their essential meaning and practice these two phrases stand for the same thing: *the nonviolent use of power. Satyagraha*, a Hindi word of Gandhi's own invention, combines two terms, *satya* and *agraha*, which together mean "soul force" or "love force." Gandhi staked his life on the belief that *satyagraha* ruled the universe. He also ardently believed that *satyagraha* could be learned and practiced by ordinary people to bring political freedom to India from British imperial domination. And it did. In 1947 Lord Louis Mountbatten left India, voluntarily and peaceably, as the last Viceroy of the British crown—forty-three years after Gandhi's first commitment to nonviolence.

Gandhi's irrepressible good humor had much to do with his effectiveness. All his biographers remark repeatedly on the twinkle of cheerfulness with which he met resistance and every challenger. When in England for a conference on self-rule for India, one of Gandhi's followers chided him for meeting with the Prime Minister and the King wearing only his loin cloth and homespun shawl. He answered the rebuke with a sly smile: "The King had on enough for both of us."

"Soul force" is the central element in his personal make-up that allowed Gandhi's religion to shape his politics. He was quoted as saying, "Those who say that religion has nothing to do with politics do not know what religion means."[1] Nonviolence cannot flourish except in a determined and ever-deepening inner life of the individual believer. Politics—the science of power in human systems—was Gandhi's vocational passion, but his nonviolence was grounded in the conviction that God is the nonviolent majesty at the heart of things, and that nonviolent resistance to violent power prevails by absorbing suffering while inflicting none in return. That belief is what drew him to the cross and resurrection of Jesus in the Christian tradition. Gandhi read through the entire Bible as a young man while studying law in England, pondering whether to leave his native Hindu faith in favor of Christianity. He warmed to the New Testament, especially to the mystical paradox of iron and eiderdown in Jesus of Nazareth—servant of the poor, challenger of the rich, debunker of the self-righteous. For Gandhi the Sermon on the Mount (Matthew 5-7) became the heart of his personal and social ethics.

Though he could not embrace some of the creedal doctrines of Christianity, he was equally distant from orthodox Hinduism, and reached out to all religions to make them his own. His regular morning and evening prayers combined readings and hymns from both the Bible and the *Bhagavad*

---

1. William L. Shirer, *Gandhi, A Memoir* (New York: Simon and Shuster, 1979), 243.

Gita (Hindu scriptures), and one of his favorite hymns was Cardinal John Henry Newman's "Lead, Kindly Light...." Gandhi's broad, inclusive ecumenism aroused the hatred of rigidly orthodox Hindus. He was assassinated by a fellow Hindu in January 1948 for insisting on the elimination of the Hindu caste of "untouchables." His death thus parallels the assassinations of others in history who have sought to bring down the rigid walls of social, racial, and religious exclusivism.

One Christmas Eve in the late 1970s I delivered the sermon in St. Philip's Cathedral, Atlanta. The church was packed to the walls with worshipers. I spoke of the moral heroism of George Washington, who endured a bleak Christmas with his underfed troops at Valley Forge, and of the sturdy grace of Robert E. Lee in remaining with his troops on Christmas Eve, even though Lee's home in Richmond was only a brief ride away. The long service ended, I stood at the main door with the Dean as the worshipers filed out. One greeting I will never forget: a young woman, her eyes flashing with anger, rebuked me for a Christmas sermon that, in her opinion, celebrated the violence of war. I was stunned. Of the countless thousands of church-door greetings in a ministry spanning nearly half a century now, that is the only one that is riveted in my memory. And I am glad for it, because it has slowly wrought a change in my soul.

Over the intervening years I have moved from the view that some violence is appropriate—as in a "just" war, or as in capital punishment—to my belief that violence is never "just" or redemptive. Though it bloodies every page of recorded human history, violence is not part of the economy of God as revealed in Jesus of Nazareth. If violence were in the arsenal of God, there would be no cross on the skyline of the world. And it is my hope that the power with which humanity has endowed violence for thousands of years to establish nations and rejuvenate cultures is gradually losing ground.

Violence continues to fascinate the human spirit, of course, and nobody profits more from this than the munitions and movie makers. But if that young woman at the cathedral door is the voice of a new world, as I think she is, the years of profiteering from violence are numbered for the weapons and entertainment industries. Think of the almost instantaneous fading of American euphoria after the Gulf War. During that brief armed conflict flags appeared on nearly half the cars in our town and George Bush's popularity rocketed to ninety-one percent. Within two months the flags had been folded and put away, and within two years George Bush was voted out of office. Consider also the prolonged reluctance of the nations to mount a counterattack against the aggressors in Bosnia and other places of conflict in the world. It is difficult to believe that the American military establishment, with its astronomical budget and enormously profitable military-industrial partnership that supplies seventy percent of the world's weaponry, can continue unabated in the face of such steadily rising resistance to war.

∞

The most remarkable feature of a developing new nonviolent mentality is its anchor in the stark centrality of the cross. A splendid analysis has been written by scholar Gil Bailie called *Violence Unveiled*. He contends that the moral basis for what was considered to be "good" violence for thousands of years began, with the crucifixion of Jesus, to unravel. With that event a revulsion against violence broke into history, with power to revise, literally to *re-vision*, the meaning of violence for those who could accept the implications of the cross. The central symbol of Christianity has the power to turn what was once good medicine into vile poison. The crucifixion of Jesus was clearly understood by those who perpetrated it as the good medicine of ritual scapegoating that restored order to a disordered society. The chief priest Caiaphas told his fellow Jews that "it is better for you to have one man die for the people than to have the whole nation destroyed" (John 11:50). This has been the underlying function of human sacrifice and the execution of prisoners from the beginning—the death of a human being as a propitiation to divine powers, or the removal of political or law-breaking prisoners judged to be threats to the safety and good order of society. Even though capital punishment was reinstituted in 1976 by our Supreme Court, the nation remains deeply ambivalent. We keep the overwhelming majority of death-row inmates in their cells, often for many years, rather than pull the switch. Culturally this seems to have the same deep meaning as the decline in the appeal of war as a problem-solver.

In the case of Jesus, the crucifixion failed to reorder the society which was disordered by the innocent victim it sacrificed. Not only did Jesus refuse to stay dead, his crucifixion aroused a counter-revolutionary empathy for the victim. This empathy began with the lament of the man in charge of the troops who did the deed: "Now when the centurion, who stood facing him, saw that in this way he breathed his last, he said, 'Truly this man was God's Son!'" (Mark 15:39). It quickly spread to the ranks of the higher authorities:

> Joseph of Arimathea, a respected member of the council,...went boldly to Pilate and asked for the body of Jesus....Then Joseph bought a linen cloth, and taking down the body, wrapped it in the linen cloth, and laid it in a tomb that had been hewn out of the rock. (Mark 15:43, 46)

Ever so slowly, the effect of this central event in the New Testament has been to withdraw legitimacy from the violence of ritual sacrifice. What had been a source of social stability for centuries was, in a single moment, shaken at its base by the crucifixion of Jesus. In the very few western societies that still impose the death penalty, executions are never carried out in public. The reason, as Bailie explains, is that executions no longer satisfy the public as rituals that restore the social order. Instead, they arouse a counter-violence that threatens the orderliness of the very society that the executions are designed to secure. Bailie recounts an ironic poem by Coventry Patmore in making his point:

> ...They brought the man out to be hanged.
> Then came from all the people there
> A single cry, that shook the air;
> Mothers held up their babies to see,
> Who spread their hands and crowed for glee....
>
> The dangling corpse hung straight and still.
> The show complete, the pleasure past,
> The solid masses loosened fast:
> The thief slunk off, with ample spoil,
> To ply elsewhere his daily toil;
> A baby strung its doll to a stick;
> Two children caught and hanged a cat;
> Two friends walked on in lively chat;
> And two, who had disputed places,
> Went forth to fight, with murderous faces.[2]

No one disputes that removing criminals and deterring would-be felons is an essential task for any society. Yet what is intended as a socially sanctioned act of violence has within

---

2. Gil Bailie, *Violence Unveiled* (New York: Crossroad, 1995), 86.

itself the power to turn its violence against the very society it seeks to protect. Something that seems entirely rational erupts into something profoundly irrational and gets so out of hand that the presumed "cure" actually becomes a "poison." In ancient Greece the victim of ritual scapegoating was called the *pharmakon*, from which comes the term "pharmacy," meaning both "medicine" and "poison." This suggests that sacrificial violence which can cure society of its distresses and disorders under some conditions can poison it under others. "More to the point," writes Bailie, "if a sacrificial event fails to function as a cure, it will inevitably function as a poison, which is what is happening in our day....Its violence begins very slowly to rebound on the society that sponsored it."[3]

The unmasking of sacred violence began on Calvary. Nothing is more important to the survival of the planet today than a vastly expanding spiritual and moral allegiance to the cross of Christ—all across the world. This could be the point that Gandhi missed about Christianity—and the point most easily missed by Christians as well. If Gandhi had seen that his *satyagraha* is at the core of the central event of the New Testament he might or might not have embraced Christianity, but he could have perceived that all religions are not the same. Only the gospel of Jesus Christ tears the veil from the face of sacralized violence, exposing its bloody offense to the love of God by arousing a permanent and irreversible empathy for the victim.

This is not to say that Christians are in any way superior to Hindus or Moslems or adherents of any of the world's religions. It is to say, however, that the *linchpin of human salvation*, individually and as a world family, is where the writers of the New Testament say it is: *in the cross of Christ.*

---

3. *Ibid.*

Peter may have been the first to say it in his testimony before an assembly of high priestly accusers early in Luke's record of the Acts of the Apostles:

> This Jesus is "the stone that was rejected by you, the builders; it has become the cornerstone." There is salvation in no one else, for there is no other name under heaven given among mortals by which we must be saved. (Acts 4:11-12)

Paul echoes this point in his letter to the Philippians:

> Therefore God also highly exalted him and gave him the name that is above every name, so that at the name of Jesus every knee should bend, in heaven and on earth and under the earth, and every tongue should confess that Jesus Christ is Lord. (Philippians 2:9-11)

The message of the cross exposes the perversity of sacred violence as destructive of the very values it is designed to guard. Violence, in all its forms, is the massive evil from which the cross of Christ delivers the soul of humanity.

This cannot mean that Jesus is owned by the Christian church, or that Christians have a monopoly on salvation. Christ is risen; Jesus is loose upon the world. As the world becomes increasingly interwoven and Christians are in dialogue with those of other faiths, several truths can wash away any remaining contempt for non-Christian religions.

The first truth is that there is simply no way one can obey the command to love one's neighbor and despise that person's deepest faith commitment. To hold another's faith in contempt is to hold that person in contempt; it is an act of violence against the soul of another. It is to behave precisely contrary to the central message of the cross: that violence, in all its overt forms of bloody brutality and all its covert forms of arrogant despising, is the massive sin from which the cross of Christ delivers the soul of humanity. Obedience to the Christ of faith is always a servanthood, and *servanthood presupposes an embracing love that looks for the lovable in others and in their religions.* William Temple held that "all that is noble in the non-Christian systems of thought and conduct is the work of Christ upon them and in them."[4]

The second truth that can win allegiance to Jesus in dialogue with other religions is to see Christian mission as part of the long struggle toward a one-world civilization. This was Temple's vision. He saw that non-Christian religions are integral parts of complex civilizations and social structures. Christian mission needs to build communities of economic justice and spiritual vitality, joining with the poor and oppressed in contending with injustice, political tyranny, and racial or tribal barriers. Redemption is social as well as personal, and experienced most fully in the context of supportive communities.

The third truth is in an admonition of Jesus that underlies all nonviolence and ratifies the cross as his crowning act of servanthood. In his agony he lived the truth he taught, forgiving his torturers and the unjust powers that conspired to do him harm.

> You have heard that it was said, "You shall love your neighbor and hate your enemy." But I say to you, Love your enemies and pray for those who persecute you. (Matthew 5:43-44)

The call to love our enemies goes to the heart of the second commandment: to reach out in love to one's neighbor. It has enormous conceptual and spiritual force—literally the power to change the world. Conceptually, to "love your ene-

---

4. Joseph Fletcher, *William Temple: Twentieth-Century Christian* (New York: Seabury Press, 1963), 133.

mies" is exactly the meaning of relinquishing the need to dominate. Loving your enemies is moving beyond the attempt to control and up to the level of the servant leader who "stoops to conquer." Max DuPree, in his landmark book *Leadership is an Art,* says it in accents that mirror the cross: "Leaders don't inflict pain; they bear pain."[5]

The practice of nonviolence in prayer and intercession for enemies—real and imagined—is to experience soul-freedom. It induces health of body and mind. It takes away rage, lets go anxiety, relaxes tension, chases fear, heightens joy, and prolongs life. Nonviolence in prayer can reach out with signals that create a nonviolent response. By the mystery of "getting back what we give" enemies can experience the deepest gift of love—the special friendship born of reconciliation. I think it was Phillips Brooks who wrote a searching line about nonviolent servanthood in prayer: "No one can be at enmity with anyone whose advocate they are before the throne of grace." This is also the inner posture of Martin Luther King, Jr., the architect of the civil rights movement:

> To our most bitter enemies we say: "We shall match your capacity to inflict suffering by our capacity to endure suffering. We shall meet your physical force with soul force. Do to us what you will, and we shall continue to love you. We cannot in all good conscience obey your unjust laws, because non-cooperation with evil is as much a moral obligation as is cooperation with good....One day we shall win freedom, but not only for ourselves. We shall so appeal to your heart and conscience that we shall win you in the process, and our victory will be a double victory."

---

5. Max DuPree, *Leadership is an Art* (New York: Dell Publishers, 1989), 11

The servanthood of nonviolence has begun to change the world. The present momentum is small, but only a minority is needed for great changes to succeed on a larger scale. Servant leaders are today's "overwhelming minority." Margaret Mead's often quoted aphorism is encouragement to all who stand on any fine frontier: "Never doubt that a small group of thoughtful, committed citizens can change the world; indeed it is the only thing that ever has."

It is the gift of God to us that there rise up prophets at critical moments, most of them from total obscurity, like Mohandas Kamarshand Gandhi. A later prophet, the playwright Christopher Fry, wrote lines in 1953 that sound today like trumpets in the morning:

> The human heart can go to the lengths of God.
> Dark and cold we may be, but this
> Is no winter now. The frozen misery
> Of centuries breaks, cracks, begins to move:
> The thunder is the thunder of the floes,
> The thaw, the upstart Spring.
> Thank God our time is now when wrong
> Comes up to face us everywhere,
> Never to leave us til we take
> The longest stride of soul man ever took.
> Affairs are now soul-size.[6]

I saw Fry's play performed in the chancel of Old St. Paul's Church in Baltimore as a young priest. I did not know then that we were hearing truth fashioned for the hinge of history on which the whole planet has begun to turn. But I know it now.

---

6. Christopher Fry, *Selected Plays: A Sleep of Prisoners* (London: Oxford University Press, 1985), 243.

The Train to Nagasaki

May the God of hope fill you with all joy and peace in believing, so that you may abound in hope by the power of the Holy Spirit. Romans 15:13

Long before there were bell-buoys and electronic navigational aids, the fishermen of a village in Scotland used landmarks on the receding shore as guides for rowing out to the fishing grounds. Facing aft as they rowed, they watched for the exact alignment of two points on the skyline: the steeple-top of the village kirk and the slowly emerging peak of the highest distant hill behind the town. They had to row far out from shore before these two points of reference precisely juxtaposed, but when they did they knew they had arrived. They deployed their gear and fished.

The story is a clue to living and leading hopefully. The word "hope" rings with the sound of tomorrow. Its meaning is future-oriented. Hope points forward from any present moment. And yet hope's finest nourishment comes from the past. History is the true source of hope. Like the fishermen in that village, we make our way forward most confidently when we can keep dependable old landmarks in sight. That is the enduring wisdom of the command that created the central act of worship in the Christian tradition: "Do this in remembrance of me." For servant leaders, whose calling is anchored in the servanthood of Jesus, his admonition to remember is the looming landmark on the shoreline of life's vast sea. Christianity is a "rowboat religion," and a rowboat is *lifeboat* size. Servant leadership is a life-giving go at life, and it rows a rowboat.

My rowboat has taken me further and further in the direction of a theology that fits my bias for the common good. My certainty is that in the next millennium the planet will support the human enterprise only as the human enterprise supports the planet. Our best support will take the form of nonviolence toward the planet's riches and toward one another as interdependent sharers of the earth. As the boundaries of nation states grow more porous, we are beginning to see that they are anachronisms, outmoded and increasingly dysfunctional in a global village created by exuberant networks of communications and finance. The human odyssey cannot continue without a quantum advance in consciousness that will build new structures of care for the earth and for one another across all boundaries.

This is not just a private view; it has become widely public, even in the churches. Research by George Gallup that concentrated exclusively on the laity of the Episcopal Church revealed that fully sixty-three percent hope for more vigorous attention to the issues of world peace by the church's clergy, and that an even greater majority—sixty-seven percent—expect far better leadership from the clergy in facing the environmental crisis.[1] These figures are, in themselves,

---

1. George Gallup, *The Spiritual Health of the Episcopal Church* (New York: The Episcopal Church Center, 1990), 21.

signs of hope. But the most significant sign of hope in my own experience is locked in a memory that goes back half a century as a personal piece of "rowboat perspective."

On October 25th of the year of the Japanese surrender in World War II, just eleven weeks after the second atom bomb was dropped by U. S. forces in 1945, I visited Nagasaki. In those few weeks since the bombing, the toll of civilian deaths rose from thirty-nine thousand (who were incinerated instantly) to something like sixty-four thousand, the difference being the count of those who died later of injuries and radiation. It is impossible to describe the devastation. The center of the city of some four hundred thousand was not reduced to the conventional rubble of ordinary bombing. Instead, the scene opened on a few square miles of brown powder and a scattering of grotesque reminders of a once thriving metropolis: a lone telephone pole, an intact plumbing fixture, half-standing chimneys. The heart of Nagasaki was simply pulverized, pock-marked by those broken leftovers.

I had traveled that day from the Japanese naval base city of Sasebo, where I was stationed on an American destroyer. Sasebo was then about a two-hour train ride north of Nagasaki on the southernmost island of Kyushu. Pulled by an ancient coal-fired steam engine, the car on which about a dozen military officers rode was the last of probably a dozen up ahead, and strictly limited to use by American and British military personnel. The forward cars were jammed with Japanese, many standing in the aisles.

On the return trip to Sasebo a few hours later, in the same exclusive kind of car, a cheerful lad of not more than fifteen was the conductor. He roamed the aisle punching our tickets. His uniform was a shiny black suit, patched at the elbows, with an old railroad cap to match, its patent leather bill bent and cracked. I was sitting alone in one of those antique arrangements of facing seats at the end of the car. When the conductor came to my place he punched the ticket and sat down opposite, smiling broadly. We were knee to knee. It turned out he wanted a cigarette, gesturing with a hand motion and blowing imaginary smoke. I offered him one from a fresh pack of Old Golds. Then he needed a light, gesturing this time as if striking a match. The act of lighting another's cigarette, with wind blowing through the open windows of a moving train, brings people's faces very close. His eyes and mine met, only scant inches apart. Unbidden in that moment tears welled up, for both of us.

Until a few minutes before we were total strangers. Until a few weeks before we were sworn enemies, separated by war, propaganda, language differences, and distant geography. But in one swift removal of all barriers, two human beings drew close in a meeting of souls. On August 14th of that fateful year the war ended. Better still, on October 25th peace came to two of us.

The implications of that vivid experience have grown large in recollection, three in particular. First, humanity is created to be a community of kinship in peace. This is the truth of life that mystical moments of reconciliation make clear, in the music that rises unbidden in our souls when souls connect—when caring and forgiveness cancel alienation, or the lilt of a birdsong awakens us to the glory of the living earth. *Relationship is our deepest longing.* We have begun to know this as scientific truth: scientists now teach us that connectedness is the foundational reality of the universe. "Cosmogenesis (the origin of the universe) is organized by communion. To be is to be related, for relationship is the essence of existence."[2] What this means, from the perception of contemporary science, is that the human soul has evolved with the longing for connection and can flourish only when nourished by it. Deeper than all our hatreds and tribal prejudices, more profound than our long attachment to war and more lasting than the world's present fearful outlay of one trillion dollars annually on the weapons to make war—stronger than all these engines of violence is a planetary pull of human longing for reconciliation and peace.

That is why all the world's religions aspire to peace at the heart of their hope. In Judaism and Christianity peace is the transcendent gift invoked by our blessings and dismissals: "The peace of God, which passes all understanding, keep your hearts and minds...." Peace is the very meaning of the word *Islam*. When its three operative consonants, S, L, and M, are combined with a variety of vowels, they spell "peace" across the whole spectrum of human speech. *Salem* is the word for peace in English. *Shalom* means peace in Hebrew, while *salaam* is peace in Arabic. In the native language of Gandhi, the word for peace is *shanti* in both Hindi and Sanskrit—often accompanied by a gesture of hands brought upright together in front of the face with a smile and a bow. Peace as a longing connects the human family in a common depth of soul. The hope for peace surges in the collective unconscious. It is for the generations now living to bring this hope to consciousness and build the structures that will give it operative vitality.

Second, the best things in life come by surprise. We do not anticipate most of the gifts that nourish us most deeply. They arrive without our contriving. I did not expect to be blessed by the smiling eyes of a nameless ambassador of friendship on a crowded train in a conquered country. Nor is the experience of enchantment with another human in the rapture

---

2. Brian Swimme and Thomas Berry, *The Universe Story* (San Francisco: HarperCollins, 1992), 77.

of love a thing that we engineer—or even anticipate. At its best, love overtakes us. "One enchanted evening," the Rodgers and Hammerstein song promised, "you will meet a stranger...." While the human will can make much history, the history worth remembering is more a matter of *meeting* than of making. The best things in life steal upon us by an energy and will not our own. Jesus was a total surprise to the prevailing cultural and religious situations of first-century Palestine—and continues to be so even now, as his kingdom vision and ethics penetrate human understanding in fresh and deeper ways.

I think this is why "mystery" has been restored to the highest place in the searches of postmodern science. It was there before the geniuses of Descartes and Newton replaced it with soul-less mechanics, but it has returned in the work of Einstein and his successors, including Brian Swimme and Thomas Berry:

> The important thing to appreciate is that the story as told here is not the story of a mechanistic, essentially meaningless universe but the story of a universe that has from the beginning had its mysterious self-organizing power that, if experienced in any serious manner, must evoke an even greater sense of awe than that evoked in earlier times at the dawn breaking over the horizon.[3]

Third, in the cosmos that humanity did not create but only inherits, new life rises from the death of the old. Death is the precondition of life: seeds must die in order for others to germinate, all forms of life must perish in order to make room for their succeeding generations. The bombs that pulverized Nagasaki and Hiroshima, taking the lives of masses of humanity, have become an axis on which the human story

---

3. *Ibid.*, 238.

turns in groping for a new direction. Those deaths have brought to birth a new resolve in the human family. From the carnage of nuclear holocaust has come the United Nations. No matter that this infant structure of global peace is the object of mixed and often hostile reviews in a world with an ancient and abiding addiction to war; though only fifty years old, the United Nations endures. It prevails as an agency of global conscience and caring, as a peace-making forum, and as a deployer for the first time in history of supra-national peacekeeping forces. Now, in order for the United Nations to be reborn as an organization that prevents wars from starting, there must die the sovereign privilege of nations to initiate war. What will bring this about? It will take much time and the multiplying of servant leaders across the world, but servanthood is the name of the power to accomplish this. As was said in the preface: "Servanthood is the way of fulfilling the human longing for peace and the planet's need of preservation as the theater of all life."

∞

The central meaning of servanthood is that great power functions as an exchange of power, never as coercion by superior forces. The universe is built this way. As the revealer of the Power that blew the cosmos into being and keeps it evolving, Jesus never coerces. Instead, it is his concise insistence by word and deed that greatness lies in giving—that superiority is embodied in serving. Persuasion is the posture of God.

Since it is the nature of sovereign nations to resist coercion, only a servanthood that exercises power as persuasion will bring about a new recognition by national sovereignties that their identities are best served in a nuclear and ecologically imperiled world by the surrender of their power to initiate war—by yielding their coercive power to the higher

authority of a self-conscious global servanthood. Such a
step, unimaginable in terms of ordinary consciousness, will
be possible only as servant leaders in all walks of life join in
seeing that the deep meaning of the axis on which history
now turns is that human evolution is on "fast forward." A
quantum advance of the planet's human consciousness is in
full flower. For fifty years following the deaths of two hundred
thousand non-combatants in Nagasaki and Hiroshima, a
whole new era of restraint has emerged. It has come upon
the world so quickly that though staggering numbers of nuclear missiles have been aimed across the old boundaries for
two generations, none has been released. And now this
weaponry is being gradually dismantled.

All this could come undone by an isolated act of human
madness, of course. So the new world now aborning will
need policing. Sin is like sewage—a built-in characteristic of
human make-up. No exertion of moral striving will banish
the reality of sin. As long as humanity is endowed with the
perilous gift of free choice there will be the need of both law
and grace, both restraint of sin and forgiveness of sin. What
is needed for hope's encouragement is to see that evolution
is not first a matter of humanity improving morally, but of
humanity rising to a higher level of consciousness—a new
awareness that awakens to the fundamental interrelated-
ness of all life and finds its fullest joy in relationships that
honor the integrity of all others. This, I believe, is the meaning of peace. And it is the true source of any higher morality—not in admonitions or promises to do better, but in the
emergence of a finer sensitivity to the dearness of the earth
and the beauty of the souls of others.

This higher consciousness explains the exalted personal
and social ethic of Jesus in the Sermon on the Mount. His
astonishing beatitudes and his call to love our enemies are
forged from an entirely new level of consciousness that Jesus

brought to the human pilgrimage, not from a pumped up resolve to be better. Jesus is the prototype of an entirely new level of evolving humanity, "the firstborn within a large family" (Romans 8:29). Jesus is the emergence within history of a quantum advance beyond *homo sapiens* (cunning humanity); he is the firstborn *hetero pacificus* (peaceable humanity), and his mission is to call into being a new population in the evolving world of God's continuous making. St. Paul heralded this event: "For anyone united to Christ, there is a new creation; the old order has gone, a new order has already begun" (2 Corinthians 5:17, REB). From this revelation we draw the empowering truth that the vocation of servanthood, in the pattern and power of Jesus, is the identifying mark of the new species which Jesus inaugurates. The vocation of servant leadership is a call to become as he was in the world—the new humanity, *hetero pacificus*—the peacemakers whom Jesus called "blessed" in his catalogue of the truly happy people.

The focus of remembrance that will nourish this advance of consciousness and cheer the human heart in hope is the central event reported in the New Testament: the new life that blossomed from the death of the Crucified. This emergence of life from death in cross and resurrection is the paradigm of enduring power—the power of servanthood that knows no limit of love. We can only guess the shape of things in the long stretch of years of the third millennium, but building hope on the memory of a cross on the skyline of the world gets us way beyond guessing and into knowing—into the persuasion that nothing "will be able to separate us from the love of God in Christ Jesus our Lord" (Romans 8:39). And from that persuasion a girding deduction follows, namely that the plausibility of hope does not come of looking ahead, but of peering aft, *as in a rowboat.*

∞

The best things in life, both private and public, are believable mostly in retrospect, not in prospect. Only in retrospect do great dreams take on the muscle of plausibility. Who has not been through a devastating loss—a job suddenly terminated or a marriage irretrievably broken—and found, by surprise on the far side of experience, that life has gained a new radiance? The principle works even more dramatically in the public arena.

Was it plausible to most of the world before it happened in April 1994 that a fiercely protective white minority holding all the power in South Africa would grant political and racial equality to an overwhelming black majority, installing as president a black leader with a record of twenty-seven years in prison as a rebel against white apartheid?

Who could have anticipated that in 1989 a seemingly invincible communism would take a week to collapse from the top, and that thirteen occupied and oppressed nations of the former Soviet Union would have achieved their freedom? Who would have guessed in the winter of 1778 that the nation founded through the efforts of a snowbound, rag-tag army of reluctant conscripts and underfed volunteers would emerge as a great nation, able to reach out from its abundance to other nations in their suffering?

Who would have thought that from the dead body of a condemned and brutalized woodworker and his cluster of intimidated disciples there would arise a band of sisters and brothers through the centuries seeking to continue his life and power, with hands of compassion and justice around the earth?

Retrospect is the key to hope, especially in the devout remembrance of a Christmas cowstall and an Easter fashioned in shape of a cross. Therefore this truth: *hope is never blind because we can see behind us.* Christmas and Easter prompt a thundering response to worship—maybe from longing for assurance that we are not alone in our hope of a finer world—a hope that needs remembrance and high ritual for its nourishment. A contemporary poet and Episcopal priest, Susan Sherard, gives voice to the persuasion that human hope is never unaccompanied by divine presence:

> Heaven will not leave us alone.
> Heaven will continue to come to earth
> Until heaven and earth are one.
> Heaven will not leave us alone until
> Love's work is done.

Resources

Servant Leadership
The Institute for Servant Leadership
The Rt. Rev. Bennett Sims, president
P. O. Box 1081
Hendersonville, North Carolina 28793-1081
(704) 697-6957   Fax: (704) 697-5386

Biography
Brown, Judith. *Gandhi, Prisoner of Hope.* New Haven: Yale
    University Press, 1989.
Fischer, Louis. *Gandhi, His Life and Message for the World.*
    New York: New American Library, 1954.
———, ed. *The Essential Gandhi, An Anthology of His Writ-
    ings.* New York: Random House, 1962
Sandburg, Carl. *Abraham Lincoln,* 6 volumes. New York:
    Scribner and Sons, 1939.
Shirer, William L. *Gandhi, A Memoir.* New York: Simon and
    Shuster, 1979.

Business and Economics
Bloch, Peter. *The Empowered Manager.* San Francisco:
    Jossey-Bass, 1987.

Breton, Denise, and Largent, Christopher. *The Soul of Economics*. Wilmington, Del.: Idea House, 1991.

Chappell, Tom. *The Soul of a Business*. New York: Bantam, 1993.

Ellul, Jacques. *Money and Power*. Downers Grove, Ill.: Inter-Varsity Press, 1984.

Fritz, Robert. *The Path of Least Resistance*. Salem, Mass.: DMA, Inc., 1984.

Galbraith, John Kenneth. *The Culture of Contentment*. New York: Houghton Mifflin, 1992.

Jones, Donald G., ed. *Business, Religion and Ethics*. Cambridge, Mass.: Oelgeschalager, Gunn and Hain, 1982.

McGregor, Douglas. *The Human Side of Enterprise*. New York: McGraw-Hill, 1960.

Novak, Michael, and Cooper, John W., eds. *The Corporation: A Theological Inquiry*. Washington, D. C.: American Enterprise Institute, 1981.

Stack, Jack. *The Great Game of Business Currency*. New York: Doubleday, 1992.

Ecology and Archaeology

Berry, Thomas. *The Dream of the Earth*. San Francisco: Sierra Club Books, 1988.

Brown, Lester R., ed. *The State of the World, 1990, 1991, 1992, 1993, 1994, 1995, 1996*. Worldwatch Institute. New York: W. W. Norton & Co.

Brueggemann, Walter, et al. *Theology of the Land*. Collegeville, Minn.: Liturgical Press, 1987.

Gore, Al. *Earth in the Balance*. New York: Houghton Mifflin, 1992.

Gould, Stephen Jay. *Wonderful Life*. New York: W. W. Norton & Co., 1989.

Leakey, Richard and Lewin, Roger. *Origins*. New York: E. P. Dutton, 1977.

McDonagh, Sean. *To Care for the Earth*. London: Geoffrey Chapman, 1986.

————. *The Greening of the Church*. London: Geoffrey Chapman, 1990.

McKibben, Bill. *The End of Nature*. New York: Random House, 1989.

Rifkin, Jeremy. *Entropy: Into the Greenhouse World*, rev. ed. New York: Bantam Books, 1989.

Swimme, Brian and Berry, Thomas. *The Universe Story*. San Francisco: HarperCollins, 1992.

Leadership

DePree, Max. *Leadership is an Art*. New York: Dell Publishers, 1989.

Gardner, John W. *Excellence*. New York: Harper and Brothers, 1961.

Greenleaf, Robert K. *The Servant as Leader*. Indianapolis: The Robert K. Greenleaf Center, 1991.

Jaworski, Joseph. *Synchronicity: The Inner Path of Leadership*. San Francisco: Berrett and Koehler, 1996.

Kotter, John P. *Power and Influence*. New York: The Free Press, 1985.

Nair, Keshavan. *A Higher Standard of Leadership: Lessons from the Life of Gandhi*. San Francisco: Barrett-Koehler, 1994.

Palmer, Parker J. *Leading from Within*. Washington, D. C.: The Servant Leadership School Press, 1995.

Wheatley, Margaret J. *Leadership and the New Science*. San Francisco: Berrett-Koehler, 1992.

Wheatley, Margaret J. and Kellner-Rogers, Myron. *A Simpler Way*. San Francisco: Berrett-Koehler, 1996.

Medicine, Psychology, and Physics

Berman, Morris. *The Reenchantment of the World.* Ithaca, N. Y.: Cornell University Press, 1981.

Bohm, David. *Wholeness and the Implicate Order.* London: Ark Paperbacks, 1983.

Capra, Fritjof. *The Turning Point.* Boston: Simon and Shuster, 1982.

———. *The Tao of Physics.* Boston: Shambhala, 1991.

Harman, Willis W. *Global Mind Change.* Indianapolis: Knowledge Systems, Inc., 1988.

Kabat-Zinn, Jon. *Full Catastrophe Living.* New York: Bantam Doubleday, 1990.

Myss, Caroline. *Anatomy of the Spirit.* New York: Harmony Books, 1996.

Sheldrake, Rupert, and Fox, Matthew. *Natural Grace.* New York: Doubleday, 1996.

Siegel, Bernie, M.D. *Love, Medicine and Miracles.* San Francisco: HarperCollins, 1986.

Walsh, Roger, M.D. "Psychiatry and the Global Crisis," a taped lecture. Topeka: The Menniger Foundation, 1993.

Theology, Ethics, and the Bible

Bailie, Gil. *Violence Unveiled.* New York: Crossroad, 1995.

Barbour, Ian. *Religion in an Age of Science.* Volume I. San Francisco: HarperCollins, 1990.

Barr, James. *Fundamentalism.* London: SCM Press, 1981.

Borg, Marcus. *Meeting Jesus Again for the First Time.* San Francisco: HarperCollins, 1994.

———. *The God We Never Knew.* San Francisco: HarperCollins, 1997.

Crossan, John Dominic. *The Historical Jesus.* San Francisco: HarperCollins, 1992.

———. *Jesus: A Revolutionary Biography.* San Francisco: HarperCollins, 1994.

Douglas, James W. *The Nonviolent Coming of God.* Maryknoll, N. Y.: Orbis Books, 1992.

Fletcher, Joseph. *William Temple: 20th Century Christian.* New York: Seabury Press, 1963.

Fosdick, Harry Emerson. *The Meaning of Prayer.* New York: Association Press, 1962.

Fox, Matthew. *The Coming of the Cosmic Christ.* San Francisco: Harper and Row, 1988.

Haughey, John C. *The Holy Use of Money.* New York: Doubleday, 1986.

Kellerman, Bill Wylie. *A Keeper of the Word: The Writings of William Stringfellow.* Grand Rapids: Eerdmans, 1994.

McFague, Sallie. *Models of God.* London: SCM Press, 1987.

————. *The Body of God.* Minneapolis: Augsburg Fortress, 1993.

McGill, Arthur. *A Test of Theological Method.* Philadelphia: Westminster Press, 1982.

Meeks, M. Douglas. *God the Economist.* Minneapolis: Augsburg Press, 1989.

Nolan, Albert. *Jesus Before Christianity.* Maryknoll, N. Y.: Orbis Books, 1976.

Pagels, Elaine. *The Gnostic Gospels.* New York: Vintage Books, 1981.

————. *Adam, Eve and the Serpent.* New York: Vintage Books, 1989.

Schillebeeckx, Edward. *Jesus: An Experiment in Christology.* New York: Crossroad, 1987.

Sheehan, Thomas. *The First Coming.* New York: Vintage Books, 1988.

Soelle, Dorothy. *To Love and To Work.* Philadelphia: Fortress Press, 1984.

Sullivan, Andrew. *Virtually Normal.* New York: Alfred Knopf, 1995.

Teilhard de Chardin, Pierre. *Science and Christ.* New York: Harper and Row, 1969.

———. *The Divine Milieu.* New York: Harper and Row, 1960.

———. *The Future of Man.* New York: Harper and Row, 1964.

Williams, James G. *The Bible, Violence, and the Sacred.* Valley Forge, Penn.: Trinity Press International, 1991.

Wink, Walter. *Naming the Powers.* Philadelphia: Fortress Press, 1984.

———. *Violence and Nonviolence in South Africa.* Philadelphia: New Society Publishers, 1987.

———. *Unmasking the Powers.* Philadelphia: Fortress Press, 1986.

———. *Engaging the Powers.* Minneapolis: Fortress Press, 1992.